Created   by the
editorial staff of ORTHO Books

Project Editor
Scott R. Millard

Writer
Michael MacCaskey

Designers
Craig Bergquist
Christine Dunham

Photographers
William Aplin
Michael Landis

# All About
# LAWNS

# Contents

# Lawns of North America

**Regionalized for the Midwest and Northeast. Answers to the most frequently asked questions about lawns.**

We think this book will be more useful to you than any other book about lawns. Why? The chapter heading above tells part of the reason, particularly the word regionalized. It means that no matter where in the Midwest or Northeast you live, Wichita, Duluth, Cincinnati, or Boston, there is something in this book for you.

The most extensive regional information is in the section, "Lawns in your area," beginning on page 80. These pages include the comments of lawn experts that live in the Midwest and North. Who knows more about the finer points of lawn growing in Illinois, for example, than an experienced individual living there?

Your climate is the single greatest factor to influence lawn growth. Climate determines whether Kentucky bluegrass or bermudagrass (or both) will thrive in your front yard. It dictates the right times to fertilize, water, and when crabgrass germinates. Diseases and weeds that are rampant in one climate are rare or nonexistent in another. It becomes easy to understand that climate is a very important reason why the information in this book is regionalized.

## National lawn survey

To find out just what kind of information people wanted in a book on lawns, we conducted an extensive survey of lawn growers and nurserymen in every part of the country. They told us of the importance of knowing the "how and when" of lawn growing. "Be

regional and practical," they said. Their most common questions are discussed in the section, "Questions... questions..." beginning on page 4.

The lawn survey told us, to no great surprise, that people care about their lawns. Many homeowners projected an unabashed pride in being able to grow a handsome lawn. We discovered that, for most, the lawn is not just a hobby. Lawns are different things to different people — a soft playground for the kids, or a pleasant backdrop for the landscape. Maybe it's the soothing color or the uniform texture that induces a lawn's appeal. Whatever the attraction, a well-kept lawn does possess a certain mystique.

## Many to thank

Without the Cooperative Extension Service offices of each state and their helpful workers, a book of this scope would not have been possible. For reference, we've listed their addresses on pages 80 to 89.

Without the help of acknowledged authorities, we could not guarantee our information as up-to-date and factual. Numerous individuals in the nursery, turf, and lawn maintenance business guided us toward the answers to everyday questions and problems that are commonplace to them.

To these many professionals, we express our appreciation.

*You don't have to tell kids about the pleasures of going barefoot, especially when it comes to playing lawn games.*

◁

*There is nothing quite like an expanse of fresh green lawn — it's the perfect backdrop for summer daydreams.*

# Questions...questions

### *"Should I have my soil tested? If so, where?"*

Soil testing reduces some of the guesswork involved in preparing a planting site. It's like any other project — eliminate possible problems before you start and success is more likely.

Most of the land grant colleges and universities will test soil samples for the residents of its state. Sometimes this is coordinated by the local Cooperative Extension Office. In states that don't offer soil testing programs, there are numerous private laboratories. Look for them in the yellow pages or ask your County Extension Agent for help.

Directions for taking a soil sample are on page 28. See also the addresses of state-provided soil testing beginning on page 80.

### *"Should I buy seed or sod?"*

Each has advantages and disadvantages. Improved varieties of cool-season grasses and warm-season grasses are frequently available as either seed or sod. A wider range of blends and mixtures is available as seed as compared to sod. St. Augustinegrass and the improved bermudagrasses are sold as sod, sprigs, or plugs and are not available as seed. Starting from seed is less expensive, but many home owners have trouble getting good establishment from a seeded lawn; the critical period of initial care is longer. Also, many weeds may start at the same time as the lawn seed. If your lawn seed was an inexpensive, low-quality mixture, weeds could possibly have been planted along with the seed (see pages 20 to 25), but more likely they were already in your soil.

Sod provides an instant lawn, is usually weed free, and of course germination is no problem. Sod can be a great help for starting a lawn on a slope (where seed can wash away), or for limited areas. For example, sod near an entryway will keep mud from being tracked inside the house.

### *"Experts use the words straight, blend, and mixture when talking about lawn seed. What should I use?"*

A *straight* is simply one type of seed of the same species and variety. An example is 'Adelphi' Kentucky bluegrass. Straights can be used for making your own mixture. Think twice, though, before planting an entire lawn with one kind of grass; disease or insect infestation can wipe it out.

A *blend* is two or more varieties of a single type of grass. A hypothetical blend of three Kentucky bluegrasses would combine 'Fylking,' 'Adelphi,' and 'Baron.' By blending, strengths are combined. A blend can produce quality, picture-perfect show lawns.

A *mixture* combines more than one species of grass per container. A typical mixture will have Kentucky bluegrass, fine fescue, and turf-type perennial ryegrass. A mixture is best for the average lawn. For most climates, they have the best insect and disease resistance, and overall adaptability.

### *"What type of grass should I buy?"*

The best advice is to plant the grass that is well-adapted in your area. The North is Kentucky bluegrass country. Take a look at page 16 for a comparison of the many improved varieties. A blend of varieties, each with desirable characteristics, makes a more adaptable, disease-resistant lawn than a single variety. Or, use a blend of Kentucky bluegrass mixed with fine fescue and turf-type ryegrass. Zoysiagrass is often recommended, but is awfully slow growing and dormant much of the year (up to 7 or 8 months), except around Long Island and south along the Atlantic Coast and in the southern edge of the midwestern states.

One tip: Look around your neighborhood for the kind of lawn you like. If you find one that is appealing, ask the owner about it. Also, pages 9 to 19 have more extensive information on the grass varieties.

### "Do I need to improve the soil if I buy sod?"

Soil preparation is the most important step in building any good lawn. Cultivate the soil as deep as possible (6 to 12 inches minimum), and add plenty of amendments (see page 28). Good soil promotes a healthy, deep rooted lawn that will need water less often. It will tend to be more resistant to attack by either disease or insects. In short, the better the soil before planting, the easier your lawn will be to take care of in the future. This is true whether you're starting a lawn from sod, seed, or any other way.

### "How soon after seeding should I mow the lawn?"

Mow a new lawn for the first time after it has grown 30 to 40 percent higher than the regular mowing height. For example, a lawn to be maintained at 2 inches should be mowed when it reaches 2½ to 3 inches.

The mower blades should be sharp; the young grass plants can be easily pulled from the soil by a dull blade. The same thing happens if the lawn is mowed when it is too tall. Our staff favors either a manual push-reel mower or rotary mower for new lawns; they are lightweight and thus safer for new grass and less disturbing to soft soil.

New lawns from sprigs, stolons, plugs, or sod should be mowed with care the first time, but are established much sooner (especially sod) and don't need the delicate treatment required of a newly seeded lawn (see pages 48 to 51).

### "How do I know when my lawn needs water?"

There are many ways to check for adequate water — visible signals, soil moisture meters, and coring tubes that actually let you see and feel the subsurface soil. Each is a guide and requires some experience and observation to employ.

Probably the simplest and most reliable signal is a change in turf color from bright green to a dull blue-green. This color change first occurs in the most drought-prone spots, especially beneath trees. Water as soon as it's noticed.

Another way of checking for water need is to take a walk across the lawn. Look to see if your footprint impressions remain visible for more than a few seconds. If the grass doesn't spring back fast, especially in the morning, water is needed.

### "How often and how much should I water my lawn?"

To avoid wasteful overwatering, wait until the lawn shows signs of needing water (see preceding question). Then water thoroughly, enough to wet the soil down to the depth of the roots, usually about 6 to 8 inches. How often your lawn needs water will depend on your climate, soil, the time of year, the type of grass you have, how deeply rooted it is, and even how high you mow.

Wetting the soil to this 6 to 8-inch depth, assuming there is no run-off, will require about an inch of water in a loam soil, more if the soil is clay, and less if it is sandy. An inch of water over 1,000 square feet is about 625 gallons. A ½-inch diameter hose 50 feet long will deliver 350 gallons per hour (50 pounds of water pressure). Thus, it would take a little less than 2 hours to water 1,000 square feet.

### "What type of mower should I buy?"

Power reel or rotary mowers are commonly used for home lawns. For either type, be certain the mowing height is adjustable to the height your lawn requires, and safety features are adequate. Older design rotaries do not have the important safety improvements of the new models. Push-reel types are the safest mowers.

The type of grass you have and the kind of lawn you want are very important considerations. Reel mowers, properly cared for, give the manicured, golf course look. They are *required* for low-growing grasses such as hybrid bermuda and bentgrass. Rotaries are better for taller growing, less intensively maintained lawns. They are also lighter weight, easier to handle than power reels, and less expensive, but they do require more frequent sharpening. See pages 48 to 51.

### "How much fertilizer does my lawn need and when should I apply it?"

A lawn's need for fertilizer depends on the type of grass, the season, and the weather. Some grasses require much more than others for proper growth. Lawn experts talk in terms of "actual" nitrogen per 1,000 square feet. For instance, a 30-pound bag of 20% nitrogen (the first number of the analysis) has 6 pounds of actual nitrogen. Pages 11 to 15 tell about the individual grasses and how much nitrogen they need.

Spring and late summer to fall are the best times to fertilize cool-season grasses. Late spring is the best for warm-season grasses. Subsequent applications through spring and into summer are determined by the amount your lawn needs and the type of fertilizer you use. Fast release fertilizers should be used sparingly (usually no more than 1 pound of actual nitrogen per 1,000 square feet) and more frequently. Slow release types can be used more heavily (up to 2 or 3 pounds of actual nitrogen per 1,000 square feet) and less frequently. See pages 52 to 55 for more information on fertilizers.

### "Should I remove clippings or let them filter down?"

There's no "yes" or "no" answer here. If your lawn is mowed often enough so that height is being reduced only one third or less, leaving the clippings should be no problem as long as they do not accumulate on the lawn surface. There are new types of mulching rotary mowers which help in dissipating clippings.

Clippings of cool-season grasses do not contribute significantly to thatch and do return some nutrients, permitting reduced fertilizer rates. But if there's a lot of clippings, they become unsightly and may suffocate grass trying to grow beneath. In such situations, removal of clippings is necessary.

### "What is thatch?"

Thatch is the layer of grass stems, dead roots and debris that accumulates above the soil and below grass blades. The name thatch is well deserved. Like the thatched roof on a tropical hut, it stops water as well as fertilizer and most everything else from reaching the soil.

Thatch is not a problem until it becomes too thick. A thatched lawn will feel spongy underfoot. Insects and disease may develop in the thatch layer, and getting enough water and fertilizer into the soil becomes difficult.

Because of their horizontal or runner-type growth habit, St. Augustine, bermuda, and bentgrass are notorious thatch formers.

Zoysiagrass and fine fescue are wiry, tough, and slow to decompose, so they also tend to form thatch. On the other hand, perennial ryegrass rarely thatches badly. See pages 57 to 59 for ways to control thatch.

### "How do I tell the difference between insect and disease damage?"

When you see a symptom such as a dead spot in your lawn, play the role of a "lawn doctor" — eliminate the most likely problems first. Spilled gasoline, fertilizer or chemical misuse, or even visits from the neighborhood dog can cause dead spots that look suspiciously like insect or disease damage.

Close examination of turf and soil will often reveal insects or where they have fed. Diseases may produce definite symptoms — spots, banding, discoloring. In many cases, grass that has died from disease is firmly attached to the ground (one exception is root and crown rot — the grass pulls up easily.) Grass killed by insect damage is often loosely attached.

Consider, also, the season. The disease that looks most like the offender may not be active at that time of year. The same is true of insects; some are at their worst in spring and fall, others in summer. See pages 60 to 79 for more on pest control.

### "How do I know crabgrass when I see it? What can be done about it?"

Crabgrass is a weed well-known by name but little-known by sight. We've heard of it being confused with other weeds like tall fescue, timothy, and nimblewill.

Take a look at the weed photographs on pages 60 to 65. You can see how crabgrass differs from the stiffly upright, tall fescue. Crabgrass blades are wider and softer than timothy blades. Nimblewill forms dense patches and is perennial (lives through winter). Crabgrass thrives wherever summers are quite hot and particularly when very moist.

Crabgrass is an annual, meaning that it completes its entire life cycle in one season. It starts brand new from seed each spring, thus the key to its control. Use what's called a "pre-emergence" crabgrass killer. This product establishes a short-lived chemical barrier on the soil which kills crabgrass seedlings just as they begin to grow. Timing is important. There are ways to kill crabgrass once it has gained a foothold, but they are much more difficult.

### "What can I do to control broadleaf weeds like chickweed, clover, and speedwell?"

Maybe you've already discovered how difficult it is to rid a lawn of these weeds. Technically, they're broadleaf and vining. They do have extensive root systems. Worse still, they are common in northern lawns.

Some seed mixes intentionally include clover because some people just like it. Make sure you want it before you plant.

The next line of defense is good lawn care. That means mowing high (2 to 3 inches for bluegrass) and fertilizing and watering correctly. Good maintenance will go a long way in avoiding weed trouble.

If necessary, use weed sprays intended for control of these weeds. Use them in spring or fall when the weeds are growing actively and temperatures are mild. See pages 60 to 65.

### "What is brown patch? Can I prevent it?"

Brown patch is really two things. One, it describes a symptom, a patch of dead grass. And two, it is the common name of a specific disease caused by the fungus *Rhizoctonia solani*. It can be confusing when the words "brown patch" are used to name both problems.

Literally, brown patch can be the result of a multitude of causes. Insects, fertilizer burn, or spilled gasoline are typical.

The fungus that causes brown patch is most damaging in transition zone areas during midsummer. Bentgrass can be severely damaged and, in the Southwest, St. Augustinegrass is often attacked. It's rare in cool summer areas such as the Pacific Northwest. Kentucky bluegrass is rarely bothered by the disease, ryegrass and fescue only moderately.

Brown patch disease is promoted by warm, humid weather. You can discourage it by fertilizing properly and by improving drainage of surface water. Several fungicides will prevent this disease. See pages 74 to 79.

# Which grass?

**This chapter is designed to help you select the grass that is right for you. Look for the one that best suits your climate, needs, and notions of what a lawn should be.**

In the following pages we've described the 15 major grasses. Some grasses are naturally better adapted to specific climatic conditions. Each grass has an area where it is *best adapted,* but this should be considered a guide, and not absolute. Note the different recommendations for mowing and fertilization rates. These two differences are a tip-off to the high and low-maintenance grasses. The grasses that require short mowing and frequent, heavy fertilization are for dedicated lawn owners only.

Another difference in upkeep lies in the way grasses spread. For instance, bermuda and zoysiagrass spread from stems that run along the ground — beneath mower height. To keep these dense and smooth, it's important to mow short. These low-growers also tend to build up thatch rapidly.

### New varieties rewrite lawn rules

The best of the improved Kentucky bluegrasses have dramatically increased disease resistance compared to common bluegrass types. Some tolerate lower mowing (to ¾ inch), compared to the 2 to 3 inches required for the older types. However, as grasses are cut lower, maintenance needs increase. The chart on page 16 describes the best Kentucky bluegrasses.

Probably the most significant breakthrough of recent years are the turf-type perennial ryegrasses. They are more persistent, more compatible

◁

*Standing on a living patchwork of experimental grasses, Bill Meyer, turfgrass specialist, notes their performances.*

with Kentucky bluegrass and fine-fescue in both color and texture, and are cleaner mowing. (Common perennial rye has frayed tips that brown after mowing.)

Turf-type ryegrass has revolutionized seed mixtures, and is now a common component. They retain the ability to start fast like common perennial ryegrass, thus have been dubbed "crisis grass" by lawn professionals. Many of the turf-type ryegrasses are described on page 17.

### The lawn business

Lawns are a big industry throughout this country, Canada, and Europe. A lot of the creeping red fescue seed planted around the world is grown in Canada. New varieties of bluegrass are being bred in Europe. Turfgrass research is carried on in several locations in this country. Tifton, Georgia, Texas A&M, Michigan State, Penn State, Rutgers University in New Jersey and areas in the Pacific Northwest are just a few of the locations familiar to the experts. Most state and land grant colleges have at least one turf specialist on staff.

At the other end of the lawn care spectrum are the lawn service companies. These companies usually contract for specific jobs which the homeowner does not want to do himself, or perhaps does not know how to do, such as weed, disease and insect control, and renovation. Fertilization is often included in their programs. Some lawn companies provide their services on a once a year basis for special jobs while others will contract for year-around lawn care.

### A lawn for your lifestyle

Of course, there can never be a perfect grass for every situation, that's why the decision as to what to plant is yours. But because of the work of the lawn experts, you can have a lawn *perfect for you.*

*The lawngrass you choose will have a great effect on the success of your lawn. Select a grass that is adapted to your area, and will match the type of use you expect it will receive. (Below: turfgrass test plot, Ohio State University.)*

# Grass climates

Below is our grass climate map. At best, all climate maps are generalities. Local conditions will vary by precipitation, temperature extremes, altitude, slope of the land, and soil types. These local characteristics, as well as maintenance practices, can play an important role in selecting a grass.

Grasses are categorized as either cool season, or warm season, according to their characteristics. Many warm-season grasses are adapted to the southern part of the United States. They grow vigorously in the warm summer months and then go dormant, turning brown with cold weather. Although better adapted to high temperatures, warm-season grasses usually aren't as hardy as cool-season grasses. Common warm-season types include bermuda, bahia, centipede, St. Augustine, and zoysiagrass. Buffalograss and blue grama are examples of warm-season grasses that can take colder climates.

Cool-season grasses are the grasses of the North. They grow actively in the cool weather of spring and fall, then grow slowly in summer heat but will remain green with ample water. Although they are primarily grown in the North, they are also valuable at higher elevations of the South.

In parts of the country with winter snow cover, active growth is in spring and fall. Kentucky bluegrass, fescue, bentgrass, and ryegrass are cool-season grasses.

Additional climate information can be found in "Lawns in your area," (see page 80). Beginning on page 11, the 15 most important lawn grasses are displayed. They are arranged in alphabetical order and each one is described in similar terms to make comparison easier.

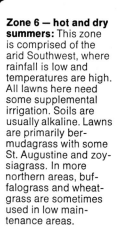

Zone 1
Zone 2
Zone 3
Zone 4
Zone 5
Zone 6
Zone 7
Zone 8

**Zone 1 — cold and humid:** This zone includes northeastern United States and southeastern Canada. It is an area of abundant rainfall and acid soils. Summers are hot and humid; winters are cold and snowy. Cool-season grasses such as Kentucky bluegrass, bentgrass, and fescue predominate. Zoysia and bermudagrass lawns are occasionally found in southern portions along the Atlantic Coast.

**Zone 2 — cold winters and summer rains:** Midwestern United States and central Canada make up this zone. Soils are not as acid and there is less rainfall compared to zone 1. Zone 2 is more acid than zone 3, but the winters are less cold. Summers are warm and humid, with frequent thunderstorms. With the exception of a few zoysiagrass lawns in the southern portion of this zone, cool-season grasses predominate.

**Zone 3 — cold and arid:** This is a large and varied zone. It is comprized of the Great Plains States, including parts of Montana, South Dakota, North Dakota, Nebraska, and Wyoming. This area is subject to drying winds in both winter and summer with relatively little rain. Here, grasses are subject to the widest temperature fluctuation in the country. Aside from cool-season grasses, natives such as buffalograss and wheatgrass are utilized because of their drought tolerance and tenacity. The intermountain area supports fine fescues.

**Zone 4 — cool and humid:** This is the Pacific Northwest, west of the Cascade Range. Rain is plentiful and soils are typically acid. Lawns are cool-season grasses and stay a beautiful green all year. Compared to the Northeast, both summers and winters are milder.

**Zone 5 — variable:** This is a transition zone that runs across the entire United States. It is in this zone that the grass climates overlap, depending on many local factors. Both warm-season and cool-season grasses are common. Selection of a proper grass type is critical, since neither cool-season nor warm-season grasses are ideally adapted in many areas. Tall fescue makes a good lawn in many areas of this zone. Good maintenance practices can make the difference between success and failure. Smart lawn owners pay close attention to the many different micro-climates around their homes.

**Zone 6 — hot and dry summers:** This zone is comprised of the arid Southwest, where rainfall is low and temperatures are high. All lawns here need some supplemental irrigation. Soils are usually alkaline. Lawns are primarily bermudagrass with some St. Augustine and zoysiagrass. In more northern areas, buffalograss and wheatgrass are sometimes used in low maintenance areas.

**Zone 7 — hot and humid:** Most lawns in this zone are made up of warm-season grasses such as bermuda, St. Augustine, and zoysiagrass. Rainfall is high and summers are warm and humid. Kentucky bluegrass may be useful in shady situations.

**Zone 8 — tropical:** This zone includes the Gulf Coast States, southern Florida, and much of Hawaii. Essentially a tropical climate, rainfall can be as high as 70 to 80 inches annually. Too much water is as much a problem here as too little water in the Southwest. In especially wet soils, carpetgrass is a good choice. Centipede, zoysia, bermuda, bahia, and St. Augustinegrass can make good lawns throughout this region.

# A gallery of grasses

## Bahiagrass

**Strengths:** Low maintenance. Extensive root system valued for erosion control and drought tolerance. Moderately aggressive.

**Weaknesses:** Forms a coarse, open lawn. Tall, fast-growing seed stalks need frequent mowing to remain attractive. Considered a weed in fine lawns. May turn yellow from chlorosis. Dollar spot and especially mole cricket may be a problem.

**Shade tolerance:** Fair to pretty good.

**Water needs:** Good drought resistance, but performs best where rain is plentiful and evenly distributed over the season.

**Fertilizer needs:** Medium, about 4 to 6 pounds of actual nitrogen per 1,000 square feet per year.

**Wearability:** Good.

**Mowing height:** High, to 3 inches.

**Best adapted:** Infertile, sandy soils. Central coast of North Carolina to east Texas. Popular in Florida.

**Varieties:** 'Argentine,' 'Pensacola.'

**Scientific name:** *Paspalum notatum*

## Creeping bentgrass

**Strengths:** The grass of choice for golf course putting greens, lawn bowling, and similar uses. Can be mowed very low.

**Weaknesses:** Requires low mowing or else it quickly builds extensive thatch layer. Creeping bentgrass, like all bentgrasses, is susceptible to several diseases.

**Shade tolerance:** Somewhat tolerant, but best in full sun.

**Water needs:** High. Poor drought tolerance.

**Fertilizer needs:** Medium to high. Needs 6 to 12 pounds of actual nitrogen per 1,000 square feet per year for highest quality.

**Wearability:** Fair to good.

**Mowing height:** Keep it low, between ¼ and one inch.

**Best adapted:** Grows without special care in sandy-loam soils of northern U.S. and Canada. Extensively used in Pacific Northwest and Northeast.

**Varieties:** 'Penncross' is quick to establish, repairs itself fast. 'Penncross,' 'Emerald,' 'Seaside,' and 'Penneagle' start from seed. From sprigs: 'Cohansey,' 'Congressional,' and 'Toronto' creeping bentgrass.

**Scientific name:** *Agrostis palustris*

## Bermudagrass

**Strengths:** Likes heat, easy to grow in most soils, takes considerable abuse. The most widely adapted warm-season grass. Tolerates little maintenance but makes a handsome lawn when given extra care.

**Weaknesses:** Invasive, poor shade tolerance, often browns in fall until spring.

**Shade tolerance:** Poor.

**Water needs:** Very drought tolerant but needs extra water in dry periods to look good.

**Fertilizer needs:** Moderate to high (4 to 12 lbs. per year per 1,000 square feet).

**Wearability:** Good.

**Mowing height:** About 1 inch.

**Best adapted:** Lower elevations of the Southwest, Maryland to Florida in the east, then west to Kansas, Oklahoma, and Texas.

**Varieties:** Common.

**Scientific name:** *Cynodon dactylon*

## Improved bermudagrass

**Strengths:** Most of the same virtues of common bermudagrass, but softer and finer textured. Generally shorter dormant season.

**Weaknesses:** More water, fertilizer, and mowing needed compared to common bermudagrass. Also more disease and insect prone. Requires regular thatch control.

**Shade tolerance:** Forget about growing it in the shade.

**Water needs:** Relatively drought tolerant but should get more than common bermudagrass.

**Fertilizer needs:** High: Up to 12 pounds or more of actual nitrogen per 1,000 square feet per year.

**Wearability:** Excellent.

**Mowing height:** ½ to 1 inch.

**Best adapted:** Very popular in the South and Southwest for a fine-quality lawn.

**Varieties:** (See chart, page 18).

**Scientific name:** *Cynodon* species

## Common Kentucky bluegrass

**Strengths:** The standard against which other grasses are measured. Looks the way most think a lawn is supposed to look—dark green, dense, with a medium texture. Easy to grow where adapted. The most important lawngrass in North America.

**Weaknesses:** Most varieties are weakened if mowed too short. Disease prone during summer periods of high heat.

**Shade tolerance:** Not too good, but certain varieties have shown some shade tolerance.

**Water needs:** High. Will recover from drought (except in semi-arid regions) as rainy season begins.

**Fertilizer needs:** Medium. Between 2 to 4 pounds of actual nitrogen per 1,000 square feet per year.

**Wearability:** Medium.

**Mowing height:** 2 to 3 inches. In summer, mow at highest level.

**Best adapted:** Grown in every northern state. Northcentral and Northeast is Kentucky bluegrass heartland.

**Varieties:** Several, see page 16.

**Scientific name:** *Poa pratensis*

## Improved Kentucky bluegrass

**Strengths:** As a group, color and density are superior to common Kentucky bluegrass. Improved resistance to diseases such as leaf spot *(Helminthosporium)*, stripe smut *(Ustilago striiformis)*, and *fusarium* blight. Some varieties take heat better; some can be mowed shorter.

**Weaknesses:** Usually higher maintenance than common Kentucky bluegrass; more fertilizer is needed and more thatch build-up.

**Shade tolerance:** Improved in some varieties.

**Water needs:** Most varieties are more drought sensitive than common Kentucky bluegrass.

**Fertilizer needs:** Medium to high. About 6 to 12 pounds of actual nitrogen per 1,000 square feet per year. Some new varieties will do well on as little as 1 or 2 pounds of nitrogen per 1,000 square feet per year if established in good soil.

**Wearability:** Better than common Kentucky bluegrass.

**Mowing height:** Check the variety list on page 16.

**Best adapted:** Same as common Kentucky bluegrass.

**Varieties:** See page 16.

**Scientific name:** *Poa pratensis*

## Centipedegrass

**Strengths:** Makes a good, low-maintenance, general purpose lawn. Adapts to poor soil. Aggressive enough to crowd out weeds. Needs less mowing than most grasses. Resistance to chinch bugs and *Rhizoctonia* disease provides an alternative to St. Augustinegrass.

**Weaknesses:** Coarse textured. Color is not dark green. Tends to yellow from chlorosis. Sensitive to low temperatures.

**Shade tolerance:** Fair.

**Water needs:** Shallow root system is sensitive to drought but recovery is fast.

**Fertilizer needs:** Low, 2 pounds of actual nitrogen per 1,000 square feet per year.

**Wearability:** Not too good. Recovers slowly from damage.

**Mowing height:** To 2 inches.

**Best adapted:** Southern U.S. The northern limit would be a line drawn between northern Alabama and Raleigh, North Carolina.

**Varieties:** 'Centiseed' is a trade name for common centipedegrass that can be grown from seed. 'Oaklawn,' developed in Oklahoma, can be established by sprigs.

**Scientific name:** *Eremochloa ophiurides*

## Dichondra

**Strengths:** Dichondra is not a grass, but a broadleaf plant. It makes a lush, dense, bright green carpet when well maintained. Needs less mowing than most grasses. Attacked by few diseases. Doesn't really have a bad season.

**Weaknesses:** Cutworms, flea beetles, snails and slugs prefer it to grass lawns. Hard to get weeds out once they invade.

**Shade tolerance:** Pretty good, better than bluegrass.

**Water needs:** High. Shallow root system cannot tolerate prolonged drought.

**Fertilizer needs:** High. Likes frequent, light feeding of ½ to 1 pound of actual nitrogen per 1,000 square feet per month during growing season.

**Wearability:** Poor.

**Mowing height:** Depends on use. In shade where traffic is rare, mow a few inches high. Lower height to about one inch is best for most other lawn areas and helps keep out weeds.

**Best adapted:** Dichondra likes heat. Not adapted to cool, foggy climates or where temperatures drop below 25°F.

**Varieties:** None.

**Scientific name:** *Dichondra micrantha*

## Chewing fescue

**Strengths:** Will tolerate close mowing in cool climate areas. Usually persistent in mixtures with Kentucky bluegrass.

**Weaknesses:** Same as red fescue. Competitiveness can be a disadvantage in mixtures with Kentucky bluegrass.

**Shade tolerance:** Same as red fescue.

**Water needs:** Low.

**Fertilizer needs:** Low. About 2 to 4 pounds of actual nitrogen per 1,00 square feet per year.

**Wearability:** Same as red fescue; may form clumps.

**Mowing height:** About 1 inch or higher.

**Best adapted:** Same as red fescue.

**Varieties:** See page 16.

**Scientific name:** *Festuca rubra commutata*

## Red fescue, creeping red fescue

**Strengths:** Frequent component of bluegrass mixtures. Blends well and does what some bluegrasses can't do — grows well in shade or drought-dry soil. Fine texture, deep green color. Tolerates acid soil.

**Weaknesses:** Very susceptible to summer diseases in hot climates, especially in moist fertile soil.

**Shade tolerance:** Usually the best cool-season grass for dry shady lawns.

**Water needs:** Good drought tolerance.

**Fertilizer needs:** Low. 2 to 4 pounds at most per year.

**Wearability:** Poor. Slow to recover if damaged.

**Mowing height:** Normally, mow 2 inches or higher. After establishment it can be left unmowed for a "meadow look."

**Best adapted:** Where summers are cool such as coastal northwest, or at higher elevations.

**Varieties:** See page 17.

**Scientific name:** *Festuca rubra rubra*

## Tall fescue

**Strengths:** A good, tough, play lawn. Some disease and insect resistance. Green all year. Good transition zone grass.

**Weaknesses:** Coarse textured, tends to clump. Not good in mixtures unless it comprises 80 or 90 percent of the mix. Must be seeded at a heavy rate.

**Shade tolerance:** Okay in partial shade.

**Water needs:** Good drought tolerance.

**Fertilizer needs:** Medium. Between 4 and 6 pounds of actual nitrogen per 1,000 square feet per year.

**Wearability:** Good in spring and fall when growth is fast. Less acceptable in summer.

**Mowing height:** Mow this one high — about 3 inches.

**Best adapted:** The best cool-season grass for transition areas. Takes heat.

**Varieties:** 'Kentucky 31.' 'Fawn' texture is less coarse. 'Alta' is wear resistant. 'Goars' most tolerant of poor soil. See chart, page 18.

**Scientific name:** *Festuca arundinacea*

## Annual ryegrass

**Strengths:** Aggressive, fast germinating, quick to establish. Best use is overseeding in warm-winter areas.

**Weaknesses:** Poor cold and heat tolerance. Doesn't mow clean. Some perennial ryegrass seed is usually mixed with annual rye, which grows in weedy clumps.

**Shade tolerance:** Medium.

**Water needs:** High.

**Fertilizer needs:** Low to medium. Between 4 to 6 pounds of actual nitrogen per 1,000 square feet per year.

**Wearability:** Medium.

**Mowing height:** Around 1½ to 2 inches.

**Best adapted:** Same as perennial ryegrass. Use for overseeding dormant bermudagrass.

**Varieties:** None.

**Scientific name:** *Lolium multiflorum*

## Turf-type perennial ryegrass

**Strengths:** Fast seed germination and establishment. Compatible in mixes with Kentucky bluegrass and fine fescues. Greater persistence than common perennial ryegrass. Cleaner mowing. Improved heat and cold tolerance. Tough play lawn.

**Weaknesses:** Suffers from winter kill in coldest climates. If it comprises more than 25 percent of a seed mix, it will impair establishment of the other grasses.

**Shade tolerance:** Medium.

**Water needs:** Intermediate.

**Fertilizer needs:** Medium. Apply between 4 to 6 pounds of actual nitrogen per 1,000 square feet per year.

**Wearability:** Fairly good.

**Mowing height:** 1 to 2 inches.

**Best adapted:** Coastal regions with mild winters and cool moist summers. Excellent for overseeding dormant bermudagrass in the South below adaptation line.

**Varieties:** See page 17.

**Scientific name:** *Lolium perenne*

## St. Augustinegrass

**Strengths:** The best warm-season lawngrass for shade. Tolerates salty soil.

**Weaknesses:** Chinch bug a serious pest. Susceptible to several diseases including St. Augustinegrass Decline (SAD) virus. Tends to thatch badly.

**Shade tolerance:** Good.

**Water needs:** High.

**Fertilizer needs:** Medium high, 4 to 7 pounds actual nitrogen per 1,000 square feet per year.

**Wearability:** Poor.

**Mowing height:** Between 1½ to 2½ inches.

**Best adapted:** Mild areas of the Southwest; Gulf Coast states.

**Varieties:** 'Floratine,' 'Bitter Blue,' and 'Floratam.'

**Scientific name:** *Stenotaphrum secundatum*

## Zoysiagrass

**Strengths:** Forms dense, fine-textured lawn, resistant to weeds. Good heat and drought tolerance. Relatively free of disease and insect pests, though chinch bugs may bother it.

**Weaknesses:** Very slow to establish. Does not thrive where summers are too short or too cool. Wiry blades tough to mow if left too long. Tends to build thatch.

**Shade tolerance:** Slow in shade but much better than bermudagrass.

**Water needs:** Good but needs more than bermudagrass.

**Fertilizer needs:** Medium-low. Between 2 and 6 pounds of actual nitrogen per 1,000 square feet per year.

**Wearability:** Outstanding.

**Mowing height:** ½ to 1½ inches.

**Best adapted:** Throughout the South. Occasionally used in the Northeast.

**Varieties:** 'Emerald' is a hybrid *(Zoysia japonica x Z. tenuifolia)* and probably the best (illustrated). *Zoysia japonica,* 'Meyer,' or 'Z-52' is much more coarse textured but more cold hardy. *Z. tenuifolia* is least cold tolerant but the finest textured.

**Scientific name:** *Zoysia* species

# The variety charts

## Varieties of Kentucky bluegrass

| Variety | Description | Strengths | Comments |
|---------|-------------|-----------|----------|
| Adelphi | Very dark green with good density and medium texture. | Good summer performance and spring greenup; widely adapted. | Good resistance to leaf spot, stripe smut and *Fusarium* blight. |
| Baron | Dark green with medium texture and density. | Moderately good summer performance and widely adapted. | Moderately good resistance to leaf spot and stripe smut. |
| Bensun (A-34) | Light green with good density and fine texture. | Good shade performance and wear resistance. A very aggressive variety. | Good resistance to stripe smut and moderately good resistance to leaf spot. |
| Birka | Moderately dark green with good density and fine texture. | Moderately good shade performance. | Good resistance to leaf spot, stripe smut, powdery mildew. |
| Bonnieblue | Moderately dark green with medium texture and good density. | Good winter color and spring greenup. | Good resistance to leaf spot and stripe smut. |
| Bristol | Dark green with a medium coarse texture and good density. | Moderately good shade tolerance. | Good resistance to leaf spot, stripe smut and powdery mildew. |
| Columbia | Moderately dark green with good density and fine texture. | Good winter color and spring greenup; moderately good heat tolerance. | Good resistance to leaf spot, stripe smut and *Fusarium* blight. |
| Delta | Medium green with an upright growth habit and moderate density. | Moderate drought tolerance. | Very susceptible to leaf spot. Prone to chlorosis in alkaline soils. |
| Fylking | Moderately dark green with fine texture. | Good sod former. | Good resistance to leaf spot, moderately resistant to stripe smut but susceptible to *Fusarium* blight. Best kept mowed 1½ inches or lower. |
| Glade | Dark green with very good density and fine texture. | Moderately good shade tolerance. | Moderately good resistance to leaf spot and good resistance to stripe smut and powdery mildew. |
| Kenblue | Medium green with an upright growth habit and moderate density. | Best at low maintenance levels — high cutting and low fertility. | Susceptible to leaf spot. |
| Majestic | Dark green with a medium texture and good density. | Good winter color and spring greenup. | Good resistance to leaf spot; moderately good resistance to stripe smut. |
| Merion | Dark green with a medium coarse texture with good density. | Good heat and drought tolerance and transplanting ability in the heat. | Good resistance to leaf spot; susceptible to stripe smut, powdery mildew, and rust. Not good in the shade. |
| Newport | Moderately dark green with medium texture and density. | Good winter color. | Susceptible to leaf spot and *Fusarium*. |
| Nugget | Dark green with very fine texture and high density; poor color in winter. | Very good cold hardiness. | Good resistance to leaf spot and powdery mildew; susceptible to dollar spot. |
| Parade | Medium green with good density and fine texture. | Good winter color and spring greenup. | Good resistance to leaf spot, stripe smut, and *Fusarium* blight. |
| Park | Moderately dark green with an upright growth habit and moderate density. | Best performance at low maintenance levels which includes high cutting and low fertility. | Susceptible to leaf spot and *Fusarium* blight. Prone to yellowing in alkaline soils. |
| Sydsport | Medium green with good density and medium texture. | Good sod former; wear tolerant, widely adapted. | Moderately good leaf spot, stripe smut, and powdery mildew resistance. |
| Touchdown | Moderate dark green with very good density and fine texture. | Moderately good tolerance of low mowing and shade; good winter color and spring greenup. | Good resistance to leaf spot, stripe smut, and powdery mildew. |
| Victa | Dark green with medium texture and density. | Moderately good summer performance; widely adapted. | Moderately good resistance to leaf spot and stripe smut. |
| Warrens A-20 | Dark green with a medium texture and good density. | Good spring greenup. | Good resistance to leaf spot and stripe smut. |
| Windsor | Moderately dark green with moderately good density and texture. | Good spring greenup. | Susceptible to stripe smut; moderately resistant to leaf spot. |

# Varieties of turf-type perennial ryegrass

| Variety | Description | Strengths | Comments |
|---|---|---|---|
| Birdie | Medium green with good density and fine texture. | Good heat tolerance. | Good resistance to brown patch; moderate resistance to crown rust. Good mowing qualities with stemming period in the spring. |
| Citation | Dark green with good density and fine texture. | Good heat tolerance. | Good resistance to brown patch; moderate resistance to red thread. Good mowing qualities. Stemming period in the spring. |
| Derby | Moderately dark green. Good density and texture. | Moderately good heat and cold tolerance. | Good resistance to brown patch; good mowing qualities. |
| Diplomat | Moderately dark green; very good density and fine texture. | Moderately good heat and cold tolerance. | Good resistance to brown patch; good mowing qualities. |
| Loretta | Light green with very good density and fine texture. | Moderately good cold tolerance and very good mowing qualities. | Good resistance to crown rust; no stemming period in spring and lower performance in the summer. |
| Manhattan | Medium green with good density and fine texture. | Good cold tolerance and good performance in the spring and fall. | Moderately good resistance to brown blight; good mowing qualities and no stemming period. |
| NK-200 | Moderately dark green with moderately good density and texture. | Good cold tolerance. | Moderately good resistance to *Fusarium* patch. |
| Norlea | Dark green; intermediate density and texture. | Good cold tolerance. | Moderately good resistance to *Fusarium* patch. Mowing quality less desirable than other varieties. Susceptible to crown rust. |
| Omega | Moderately dark green with good density and texture. | Moderately good heat and cold tolerance. | Good resistance to brown blight and moderate resistance to brown patch. Good mowing qualities with short stemming period. |
| Pennfine | Moderately dark green with good density and texture. | Good heat tolerance. | Good resistance to brown patch and moderately good resistance to brown patch. Good mowing qualities with stemming period in the spring. |
| Regal | Dark green with moderately good density and texture. | Moderately good heat tolerance. | Moderately good brown patch resistance. Moderately good mowing qualities. |
| Yorktown I | Dark green with good density and texture. | Moderately good heat and cold tolerance. | Moderately good brown patch and brown blight resistance. Good mowing qualities. |
| Yorktown II | Dark green with very good density and fine texture. | Moderately good heat and cold tolerance. | Good resistance to brown patch and crown rust; very good mowing qualities. |

# Varieties of fine fescues

| Variety | Description | Strengths | Comments |
|---|---|---|---|
| Banner | Chewings type, dark green, good density and fine texture. | Moderately good disease resistance and tolerant of close mowing. | Very competitive with Kentucky bluegrasses in mixtures. Susceptible to powdery mildew. |
| Boreal | Creeping type, moderately dark green. Medium texture and density. | Good seedling vigor. | Has good winter hardiness. |
| Cascade | Chewings type. Medium green with very fine texture. | Good establishment rate. | Susceptible to leaf spot. |
| C-26 | Hard fescue type, dark green, fine texture, and good density. | Good disease resistance compared to the other fine fescues. Good drought tolerance. | Should perform well in mixtures with Kentucky bluegrass. |
| Dawson | Semi-creeping type, medium green, good density and fine texture. | Moderately good leaf spot resistance and tolerant of close mowing. Good for overseeding bermudagrass. | Can be damaged severely by dollar spot. |
| Fortress | Creeping type forming extensive rhizomes. Dark green with medium texture and density. | Good resistance to powdery mildew and good seedling vigor. | Blends well with Kentucky bluegrasses and recovers well from summer injury. |
| Highlight | Chewings type. Medium green with fine texture and good density. | Moderately good disease resistance and tolerant of close mowing. | Very competitive with Kentucky bluegrass in mixtures. |

*(Chart continued on page 18)*

## Varieties of fine fescues, continued

| Variety | Description | Strengths | Comments |
|---|---|---|---|
| Illahee | Creeping type. Dark green, medium texture and density. | Good seedling vigor. | Blends well with Kentucky bluegrasses. |
| Jamestown | Chewings type. Dark green, good density and fine texture. | Moderately good disease resistance and tolerant of close mowing. | Very competitive with Kentucky bluegrass in mixtures. Susceptible to powdery mildew. |
| Pennlawn | Predominantly a creeping type. Medium dark green, good density and fine texture. | A widely adapted variety with moderate disease resistance. | Used widely in mixtures with Kentucky bluegrasses. |
| Ruby | Creeping type. Dark green, medium texture and density. | Good seedling vigor. | Blends well with Kentucky bluegrasses. |
| Wintergreen | Chewings type. Moderately dark green, fine texture and good density. | Good winter color and rust resistance. | Good winter hardiness, used in northern areas. |

## Varieties of tall fescue

| Variety | Description | Strengths | Comments |
|---|---|---|---|
| Alta | Upright growing and coarse texture. Medium green. | Drought tolerant. Moderately persistent in turf. | Has performed equal to Kentucky 31 in Northern California. |
| Fawn | Upright growing and coarse texture. Medium green. | Drought tolerant. | Susceptible to crown rust. Not as persistent in turf as Alta and Kentucky 31. |
| Goar | Upright growing and coarse texture. Medium green. | Drought tolerant. | Lacking competitive ability compared to Alta and Kentucky 31. |
| Kentucky 31 | Coarse texture and somewhat lower growing than Alta and Fawn. Medium green. | Drought tolerant. Widely adapted to many soil types. Moderately disease resistant. | Good persistence in turf in transition zone. Good winter recovery and spring green up. |
| Kenwell | Slightly lower growing than Kentucky 31 with coarse texture. Medium green. | Drought tolerant. Better fall color than Kentucky 31 in fall. | Similar to Kentucky 31 with slightly better disease resistance. |

## Northern native grasses

| | Description | Culture | Comments |
|---|---|---|---|
| American beachgrass (Ammophila breviligulata) | A tough grass that grows tall, to about five feet. Deep root system and aggressive underground runners allow rapid growth and spread in shifting, infertile beach sand. Very similar to European beachgrass but has a longer planting season and greater persistence. | Dig old clumps in fall just before complete dormancy. Cut stems back to about two feet. Plant clumps about eight inches deep. Addition of fertilizer at planting time will promote more rapid growth. | Used for first-stage stabilization of shifting dune areas. As soon as the grass covers, begin planting more permanent woody plants. Beachgrass grows naturally on the shores of the Great Lakes, along the Atlantic Coast from Newfoundland to North Carolina and along the Pacific Coast. |
| Blue grama (Bouteloua gracilis) | Grayish green and fine-textured. Excellent heat and drought tolerance. Used in rangeland seedings or similar never-water situations. | Use 1 to 3 pounds of seed per 1,000 square feet. Sow fall or spring, about 30 days to germination. Mow to 2 or 3 inches. Very little fertilizer required. | Basically a warm-season grass but hardy to −40°F. An important native of the Great Plains, it's found in Wisconsin, Manitoba, Alberta, and south to Arkansas. Good in arid-alkaline soil. |
| Buffalograss (Buchloe dactyloides) | Fine textured blades are grayish green. One of the most dominant grasses of the short-grass prairie. Grows during summer and has outstanding heat tolerance. Only green during growing season which is often short. | Easily started from seed. Use 3 to 5 pounds per 1,000 square feet in fall. Should come up in about 30 days. Water deep to establish, then little is needed. Give ½ to 2 pounds of actual nitrogen per 1,000 square feet per year. Mow to about 1 inch. | Favored by settlers for building sod houses, it makes a dense turf. Thrives in areas that receive 12 to 25 inches of rain per year (Minnesota to central Montana; south to Iowa, Texas, Arizona, and northern Mexico). Does well in heavy soil. |
| Fairway wheatgrass (Agropyron cristatum) | Not a true native — introduced from Russia. Very tolerant of high temperatures, takes up to 110°F. Okay in cold to −20°F. and lower. Related to the nuisance weed, quackgrass. | Sow 3 to 5 pounds of seed per 1,000 square feet. Germination in 14 to 30 days. Water deeply until established then no supplemental water should be necessary. Mow to 2 inches. | Grows best in moist alkaline soil. Commonly found throughout much of western Canada, the northern Great Plains, and other northern mountain regions of the U.S. Sometimes grows as far south as Texas and as west as northeast California, Oregon, and Washington. |

Native grasses make excellent low-maintenance ground covers. They don't make the most attractive home lawn, but can be used to stabilize banks, and roadsides. Fertilizer and water needs are minimal. Growth is slow, so mowing is usually done three or four times per season. Some native grasses may be difficult to find, but if they are adapted to where you live and are useful in your area, they will be available. Check with your nurseryman or local seed supplier.

# Lawngrass comparisons

The following lists compare the specific types of grass in general terms. They are based on the personal observations of many specialists, and are not absolute. The specific qualities of one grass could vary, and newly developed varieties may enter at different positions in the lists.

A particular grass type may seem perfect for your home lawn. However, there are many other factors you should take into consideration, such as adaptation to your climate and maintenance requirements. For instance, where warm-season grasses are best adapted, the cool-season grasses naturally drop out of the lists and vice versa.

## High temperature tolerance

**Tolerant**
zoysiagrass
improved bermudagrass
common bermudagrass
St. Augustinegrass
centipedegrass
bahiagrass
buffalograss
tall fescue
Kentucky bluegrass
perennial ryegrass
colonial bentgrass
creeping bentgrass
roughstalk bluegrass
**Intolerant**

High temperature tolerance depends on variety and maintenance practices, and a whole range of climatic factors that affect growth habits. Raising the cutting height of a cool-season grass will improve its temperature tolerance. Also, tolerance to high temperatures is more important in transitional areas, since the grass is not as well adapted.

## Accepts low mowing

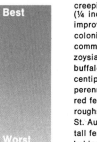

**Best**
creeping bentgrass (¼ inch or less)
improved bermudagrass
colonial bentgrass
common bermudagrass
zoysiagrass
buffalograss
centipedegrass
perennial ryegrass
red fescue
roughstalk bluegrass
St. Augustinegrass
tall fescue
bahiagrass
**Worst**

Mowing height is primarily determined by the growth habit of the grass. Those that spread horizontally can be clipped lower. There are certain cool-season varieties such as 'Merion' Kentucky bluegrass that can be cut at ¼ inch to ⅜ inch for backyard putting greens, but this is seldom recommended. In general, Kentucky bluegrass cut above 1½ inches is much easier to keep.

## Drought tolerance

**Best**
bahiagrass
improved bermudagrass
zoysiagrass
buffalograss
common bermudagrass
blue grama
crested wheatgrass
tall fescue
red fescue
centipedegrass
St. Augustinegrass
colonial bentgrass
dichondra
creeping bentgrass
roughstalk bluegrass
Kentucky bluegrass
perennial ryegrass
**Worst**

A grass may tend to remain green and resist short periods of drought. However, this same grass may, if subjected to severe drought, die out completely.

## Fertilizer requirements

**A little**
buffalograss
red fescue
bahiagrass
zoysiagrass
tall fescue
centipedegrass
St. Augustinegrass
perennial ryegrass
Kentucky bluegrass
roughstalk bluegrass
common bermudagrass
improved bermudagrass
dichondra
colonial bentgrass
creeping bentgrass
**A lot**

While a lawn may exist on rather low amounts of fertilizer, high or desirable quality may only come with increased amounts. The variety, kind of soil, and climate greatly influence fertilizer needs.

## Disease resistance

**Best**
tall fescue
zoysiagrass
buffalograss
improved bermudagrass
common bermudagrass
bahiagrass
St. Augustinegrass
perennial ryegrass
centipedegrass
red fescue
Kentucky bluegrass
roughstalk bluegrass
dichondra
colonial bentgrass
creeping bentgrass
**Worst**

A grass may be indicated as having few disease problems, but this chart represents composite knowledge of the overall disease situation. Under the right environmental conditions, a single disease may be quite devastating.

## Shade tolerance

**Tolerant**
red fescue
St. Augustinegrass
roughstalk bluegrass
dichondra
colonial bentgrass
tall fescue
creeping bentgrass
bahiagrass
centipedegrass
perennial ryegrass
Kentucky bluegrass
zoysiagrass
buffalograss
improved bermudagrass
common bermudagrass
**Intolerant**

Shade tolerance of turf depends upon many conditions. If the site is quite damp, roughstalk bluegrass could persist while red fescue would die out completely. On a dry site it would be the opposite. There often are also significant varietal differences.

## Establishment time from seeds or stolons

**Fast**
improved bermudagrass (stolons)
common bermudagrass
perennial ryegrass
creeping bentgrass (stolons)
St. Augustinegrass
roughstalk bluegrass
bahiagrass
centipedegrass
tall fescue
bentgrass (seed)
buffalograss
red fescue
Kentucky bluegrass
dichondra
'Emerald' zoysiagrass
**Slow**

The point at which a new planting becomes a lawn depends upon the lawn owner. If it is only for appearance, and to keep the soil in place, a new seeding of perennial ryegrass or tall fescue (at a heavy rate) can do the job, in as little as 2 to 3 weeks.

## Wearability

**High**
zoysiagrass
improved bermudagrass
bahiagrass
common bermudagrass
buffalograss
tall fescue
Kentucky bluegrass
perennial ryegrass
red fescue
St. Augustinegrass
centipedegrass
colonial bentgrass
creeping bentgrass
roughstalk bluegrass
dichondra
**Low**

In many situations traffic is much more than any turfgrass can tolerate. Again, there is quite a lot of varietal variability. 'Benson,' 'Baron,' and 'Merion' Kentucky bluegrass take traffic rather well.

# Lawn seed – from the ground up

Seed is the most common way to start a new lawn. Years ago, what was swept from the barn could be scattered around the yard and eventually, a lawn would grow. This casual and haphazard approach has been superceded by a very sophisticated industry that supplies around 120 million pounds of lawn seed to grow turf each year.

Of the millions of pounds of seed produced, Kentucky bluegrass is the most important. It is the most widely adapted grass of North America. Common bermudagrass is also planted in large quantities, with fine and tall fescue and the ryegrasses being the other important lawn seeds.

Seed is a popular method to start lawns, partly because it's economical. Computing the total expense of a new lawn, the seed is usually no more than five percent of the total cost.

Seed quality is important. Quality seed is healthy, with a high percentage of germination. It is also weed and disease free. A few more dollars for five pounds of the highest possible quality seed for example, can save hundreds of dollars in the years ahead. You'll have fewer weed and disease problems and will generally have a higher quality lawn.

## The keys to starting with seed

Experience has shown that the type of seed you select is very important. Make sure the grass type and variety are adapted to your area. Read the label on the seed container carefully. Prepare the soil well and ensure good contact between the seed and the soil when planting. Sow the seed at the time of year most favorable to germination (see pages 27 to 31). Keep the new seed bed moist until after germination. Be certain you have the answers to these important questions before you purchase the seed.

☐ Will your lawn be used primarily for decoration or for recreation?

☐ Which grasses are best adapted to where you live?

☐ Will the lawn be partially shaded or receive full exposure to the sun?

☐ How much time and energy are you willing to put into lawn care?

These questions may seem obvious, but they are very important considerations. Most can be answered by referring to the descriptions of the grasses on the previous pages.

## Good seed doesn't cost, it pays

Although some aspects of lawn seed production are under state and federal regulations, the seed producers desire for quality is the only sure guarantee of good seed. But by knowing how to read a seed label, many comparisons can be made that will help you make a better decision.

The variety of boxes and containers of lawn seed available in most garden centers and hardware stores can make selecting lawn seed a bewildering experience. Besides the color and size of the box and a brand name, there is no way to compare value other than reading the label.

Seed box labeling is government regulated. The Federal Seed Act of 1939 determines the basic structure of seed labels. Many individual states have their own seed labeling laws but any variance from the federal standard is usually insignificant.

There is no real mystery to seed labels, but because of government regulations and the use of a technical vocabulary, they can be difficult for the casual or beginning gardener to understand. Seed labels are a legal document; each word has a specific meaning.

The sample seed label illustrated on the opposite page shows and briefly explains the major parts of a typical label. The following is a more detailed account.

## Understanding a seed label

**Directions for use:** Most commercial mixes will tell you how much seed to use and sometimes when to seed. Some will indicate the spreader setting to use.

The spreader setting is merely a guide, although usually an adequate one. A statement like "enough seed for 1,000 square feet of new lawn," is better. You then know how far the seed will go, regardless of how you intend to spread it.

Experts have determined how many seeds per square inch are best for new seedings. These rates will vary according to many factors, such as the seed size and the growth habit of the grass. But most lawns get a good start if seeded at a rate of approximately 20 seeds per square inch — just less than 3 million seeds per 1,000 square feet. (These figures certainly are not intended to be precise and only serve as an example.) Some quick multiplication will show that 3 million seeds per 1,000 square feet is the same as 1½ pounds of Kentucky bluegrass per 1,000 square feet or 5 pounds of fine fescue over that same area. For more on this, take a look at "Seed facts" on page 23.

It is interesting to note that different varieties of the same type of grass will vary in seed size. However, the difference is inconsequential when determining application rates. For example, 'Sydsport' Kentucky bluegrass has 1,800,000 seeds per pound, while 'Birka' has only 1,380,000 seeds per pound.

*To recreate the "shades of shade" found around the home, shade cloths of varying densities are placed above test grasses. Turf researchers then record the respective tolerances.*

Naturally, the quantity recommended to sow is based on average conditions. If you expect a lot of the seeds to be eaten by birds, or otherwise fail to survive past germination, sow at a heavier rate. But seeding heavily just to be generous is not always a good idea. Grasses planted too closely together will produce weaker plants that are slower to mature.

**"Fine-textured" and "Coarse":** The fine-textured grasses are the backbone of a high quality lawn seed mix. Kentucky bluegrass and the fine fescues are the most important fine-textured types.

Bentgrasses are also considered fine-textured. At one time, they were a component of all quality mixes. They are soft and their narrow leaf-blades qualify them as fine textured, but because of their different growth habit and management needs, they do not mix well with Kentucky bluegrass, fine fescue, or turf-type perennial ryegrass. They form unattractive clumps in a bluegrass lawn if the lawn is mowed high. Mowed low, the bentgrass will eventually predominate anyway because the others will be crowded out. Alone and properly cared for, the bentgrasses can make a handsome lawn.

Bluegrasses other than Kentucky types *(Poa pratensis)* are also legally considered fine-textured. Rough-stalk bluegrass *(P. trivialis)* is found in some shady lawn mixes. Bermudagrass is also listed as fine-textured. All other grasses must, by law, be listed as "Coarse."

Specifically, the coarse grasses are tall fescue, meadow fescue, redtop, timothy, and both annual and perennial ryegrass. However, considering the ryegrasses in this category is a bit problematical. It is true that annual and common perennial ryegrasses are wide bladed, clump forming, coarse grasses. But the new varieties of perennial ryegrass, called "turf types," are as fine-bladed as Kentucky bluegrass. These turf-type ryes are premium quality lawngrasses, some labeled as fine-textured, others unfairly labeled as coarse. Thus, it is

# Reading a seed label

This label is an example of what you will find on the shelf at your garden store. The proportions of the actual grasses listed are only a sample. The low percentages of weed and crop seed, the absence of noxious weeds, and the high germination percentages indicate a high quality mixture.

These are the backbone of quality lawns, the common high-quality grasses, such as Kentucky bluegrass and fine fescue.

Look for named varieties. They're considered superior to common types, and in most cases are a sign of quality.

This percentage is the proportion of the grass by weight, not seed count. See "Seed facts" page 23.

Generally, "coarse kinds" tend to clump and don't mix well with other grasses. If there are any listed, they should not total more than 50% (One exception are the turf-type ryegrasses. By law, some are listed as coarse, but they are actually fine-textured.)

It's virtually impossible to keep all weed seeds out of a crop, but look for less than 1 percent. Weeds included here are regulated by state law.

Where the seed crop was grown must be shown for seed quantities greater than 5% of the mixture. This has no bearing on adaptation of the grass.

This is the quality most subject to change, for the worse, as the seed ages. It represents the percent of viable seed that will germinate under ideal conditions. This varies with the grass.

These are seeds of any commercially grown crop. They may be other turfgrasses, or real problems, like timothy or orchardgrass. Look for "zero crop seed" or as close as possible.

| Fine-textured Grasses | Origin | Germination |
|---|---|---|
| 30% Kentucky bluegrass | Oregon | 87% |
| 20% Merion Kentucky bluegrass | Oregon | 91% |
| 20% Fylking Kentucky bluegrass | Oregon | 90% |
| 29% Creeping red fescue | Canada | 95% |

| Coarse Kinds | Other Ingredients |
|---|---|
| None claimed | 0.01% Crop seed |
| | 1.05% Inert matter |
| | 0.03% Weed seed |
| | No noxious weeds |
| | Tested: Within 9 months of today's date. |

All the chaff, dirt, and miscellaneous matter that manages to escape cleaning is inert matter. It's harmless, but shouldn't total more than 3 or 4 percent.

Noxious weeds are the most troublesome. In most states, it is illegal to sell seed that contains certain noxious weeds. They must be individually named and the number of seeds per ounce indicated. Quality seed should have none.

This is the guarantee of other information, particularly percent germination. Current dates are best, but seed stored in a cool, dry place will last months longer.

Germination percentages let you know how many of each seed type will germinate under ideal conditions as of the test date. By multiplying the percent germination and the percent of the grass type in the mixture, you can determine how many seeds of that type have the potential to grow. This is called "percent-pure live seed." This percentage is not listed on the label, but it's one way, although complicated, to figure the real value of the seed before purchase.

Let's go back to our sample of 60% bluegrass and 40% fine fescue mixture. If the germination percentage of the bluegrass is 80%, then 60% multiplied by 80% (.60 x .80) equals the percent-pure live seed of Kentucky bluegrass. Usually 90% of the fine fescue will germinate. So, 90% multiplied by 40% equals the pure live seed of fescue in the mixture. In these terms the mixture is actually 48% Kentucky bluegrass and 36% red fescue. Obviously, as the germination percentage goes down, you are buying less viable seed.

If a container of seed is unmixed and unblended, it will list the percent "purity." Essentially, this has the same meaning as the percentage of grass types in a seed mixture mentioned earlier. A box of straight Kentucky bluegrass should be at least 90% pure. Again, by multiplying the percent purity by the germination percentage, you can determine how many viable seeds are in the box, thus the value of the seed.

Percent-pure live seed is a good way to compare value but is not the

*Rust disease can be devastating to seed growers; naturally resistant varieties are valued.*

apparent that the term coarse can be misleading, and can cause problems. If you know something about the seed in the box and its potential, you can be the best judge.

**Percentages:** When the label says that 60% of a given mixture is Kentucky bluegrass and 40% is red fescue, it means 60% and 40% by *weight* of the contents. If the meaning of this is not apparent, take a look at "Seed facts." Note that there are usually over 2 million seeds of

Kentucky bluegrass in a pound, and approximately 600,000 seeds per pound of red fescue. When you plant a mixture labeled as 60% Kentucky bluegrass and 40% red fescue, in actual seed numbers you are planting 84% bluegrass and 16% red fescue. A red fescue seed weighs three times more than a seed of Kentucky bluegrass. The actual contents of a seed mixture would be more apparent if the percentages were in seed counts, rather than weight.

*Here's how a breeder makes a quick field check of a grasses' seed production. The seed heads are removed from the plant (left), and gently rubbed between the palms (center). The seed easily separates from the hulls (right).*

only measure. In terms of the label, judge quality primarily by comparing percent germination, percent weed and crop seed, and the occurrence, if any, of noxious weeds.

**"Crop" and "Weed" seed:** Plants that are considered crop and those considered weeds are distinguished by agricultural laws of individual states. Keep in mind that labeling laws were designed for farmers, not buyers of lawn seed. That's why some of the most serious lawn weeds may not be listed under "Weeds." Timothy, orchardgrass, tall fescue, and bromegrass — all serious lawn weeds — are usually classified as crop. Just 1% of a weedy fescue can contribute 10,000 seeds to every 1,000 square feet of new lawn. Both timothy and redtop have small vigorous seeds. A small percentage of these can produce many established weeds in the new lawn.

Consider likewise, the percentage of weed seeds. The percent could represent a few large, harmless weeds, or many serious lightweight weed seeds. The quality of the producer is the only standard to judge by. At a 0.27% weed percentage, for instance, a homeowner can plant 30 unwanted chickweed seeds per square foot.

**"Noxious" weeds:** These weeds are often difficult to eliminate once they're established. Many spread just as aggressively with runners or bulbs as by seed. Each state will have a list of weeds considered noxious.

The specific noxious weeds as set forth by the Federal Seed Act are: whitetop (*Lepidium draba, Lepidium repens, Hymenosphysa pubescens*); Canada thistle (*Cirsium arvense*); dodder (*Cuscuta* sp.); quackgrass (*Agropyron repens*); johnsongrass (*Sorghum halepense*); bindweed (*Convoulus arvensis*); Russian knapweed (*Centaurea picris*); perennial sowthistle (*Sonchus arvensis*); and leafy spurge (*Euphorbia esula*). These are primarily field crop weeds, but a few are serious lawn weeds.

Annual bluegrass (*Poa annua*) and bermudagrass are noxious weeds in a few states. If present in a seed mixture, noxious weeds must be named and the number of seeds per ounce shown. In a quality seed mixture, there should be none.

## Straights, mixes, and blends

The word "straight" is used to describe lawn seed composed of just one type of grass. Many warm-

# Seed facts

| Name | Use | No. seeds per lb. | Lbs. seed per 1,000 sq. ft. | % purity | % germination | Days to germinate* |
|---|---|---|---|---|---|---|
| **Bahiagrass** | Low maintenance. Gulf Coast. | 175,000 | 8 | 75 | 70 | 21-28 |
| **Bentgrass, creeping** | Putting/bowling greens. Cool moist climates. | 6,500,000 | 1 | 98 | 90 | 4-12 |
| **Bermuda, common** | Good play lawn. Most important grass of southern states. | 1,750,000 | 2 | 97 | 85 | 7-30 |
| **Blue grama** | Low maintenance, drought tolerant. Northern Plains. | 800,000 | 2 | 40 | 70 | 15-30 |
| **Bluegrass, Kentucky** | Widely adapted, all-purpose. | 2,200,000 | 1½ | 90 | 80 | 6-30 |
| **Buffalo-grass** | Central Plains, tough, drought tolerant, low maintenance. | 290,000 | 5 | 85 | — | 20-30 |
| **Carpetgrass** | Tropical, wet soils, low maintenance. | 1,300,000 | 2 | — | 90 | 21 |
| **Centipede-grass** | Gulf Coast, low maintenance. | 410,000 | ½ | 50 | 70 | 14-20 |
| **Dichondra** | Southwest. Lawnlike ground cover. | | 1 | | | 14-24 |
| **Fescue, fine** | Widely adapted. Tolerant of shade. Takes dry soil. | 615,000 | 5 | 97 | 90 | 5-10 |
| **Fescue, tall** | Good transition zone grass. Tough play lawn. Use by itself. | 230,000 | 12 | 97 | 90 | 7-12 |
| **Ryegrass, annual** | Quick cover for winter overseeding. | 230,000 | 9 | 97 | 90 | 3-7 |
| **Ryegrass, perennial** | Improved types called "crisis grass." Good in mixes. Common kinds coarse and clumpy. | 230,000 | 9 | 97 | 90 | 3-7 |

*Varies according to growing conditions

season lawns are unmixed and unblended with other grass types. Lawns of common or improved bermuda, St. Augustine, or zoysiagrass are examples. Tall fescue and bentgrass are cool-season grasses that are sometimes used alone. For most cool-season lawns, a mixture or blend is preferred.

A mixture contains different varieties of seed which adjust individually to the varying soil conditions and sun or shade areas of typical lawns. The strength of one grass type compensates for another's weakness. A lawn of a single variety of Kentucky bluegrass could be wiped out if a potent disease swept through. With considerable amounts of fescue or rye in the lawn, the effect of the disease is lessened.

In the past, a little bit of everything was thrown into a bag of lawn seed. It was the shotgun approach — grow-

ers weren't too sure what was going to work so a little of everything was tried.

Also, some still speak of the "nursegrass" in a mixture. The idea of a nursegrass, disregarded today, is that a hardy, fast-growing grass makes the way a little easier for the slower, more delicate premium grass. We now know the fast grasses actually compete too much with the others and slow establishment of the premium grass.

The grasses that mix together best will have similar color, texture, and growth rate. They will be roughly equal in aggressiveness. The most important grasses that are similar in these respects are Kentucky bluegrass, fine fescue, and the turf-type ryegrasses. Seed formulators vary the relative amounts of these ingredients and sometimes add small amounts of other grasses, depending upon the intended use of the mixture. For instance, more fescue will be added if the lawn will be partly shaded or if the soil is drought prone. More turf-type ryegrass will get the lawn off to a fast start. More Kentucky bluegrass will produce the show lawn. Opinions of many experts and regional considerations also play an important part in making up a seed mixture.

Many good packaged lawn seeds are a combination of a mixture and a blend. A blend is a combination of varieties from one species. Characteristically, a blend is between a regular mixture and a straight. Resistance to particular diseases are somewhat improved and there is a look of consistency in texture and color. Seed containers that announce something like "an all-bluegrass mixture" are technically blends.

## Measures of extra-quality seed

Almost every state has a program of seed certification. Technically, "certified" seed only guarantees varietal purity. In other words, if the label says "Certified 'Adelphi' Kentucky bluegrass," the contents of the bag are guaranteed to be 'Adelphi' Kentucky bluegrass.

In most states certified seed also ensures higher overall quality. Fewer weed seeds and other crop contaminates, as well as less inert filler are also guaranteed.

"Percent fluorescence" is a special rating of perennial ryegrass. The photographs on this page show what fluorescing seed looks like. In 1929, it was discovered that annual ryegrass secreted a fluorescent substance when it was germinated on white filter paper. By contrast, the improved, turf-type ryes secrete none of this substance.

A simple way to test for contamination of improved ryegrass is to germinate a sample on filter paper. If there is any fluorescence when exposed to ultraviolet light, the presence of annual ryegrass (or a hybrid of annual and perennial ryegrass) is established. To date, only the Manhattan Ryegrass Growers Association requires this test of quality to be indicated on the seed tab, by calling the fluorescing seedlings "Other crop."

## Germination to establishment: how long?

It will be repeated several times in this book that post-seeding care, especially watering, is the single most important factor in deciding the success or failure of a seeded lawn. The trick is to water enough to keep the soil moist, but not so much the soil washes away. This delicate nurturing period, when watering can be a several-times-a-day chore, extends between the time the seed is sown and the point when the grass becomes established. You might wonder how long this period will last? The answer to this question depends on the type of grass, its rate of germination, and initial growth, and the daily temperature. To illustrate this, we conducted an experiment at the Ortho Test Garden in St. Helena, California.

Four grasses were sown the same day: 'Manhattan' perennial ryegrass, 'Merion' Kentucky bluegrass, 'Fortress' creeping red fescue, and common bermudagrass. The photographs at the right, taken at 15 day intervals, show what happened.

Actually, the rate of germination surprised us. The 'Manhattan' ryegrass came up in less than five days. The others were also faster than expected. This extra fast germination was probably due to an unexpected heat wave during the first week that sent temperatures into the mid-nineties. Seed invariably germinates more slowly in the cool temperatures of late fall or early spring.

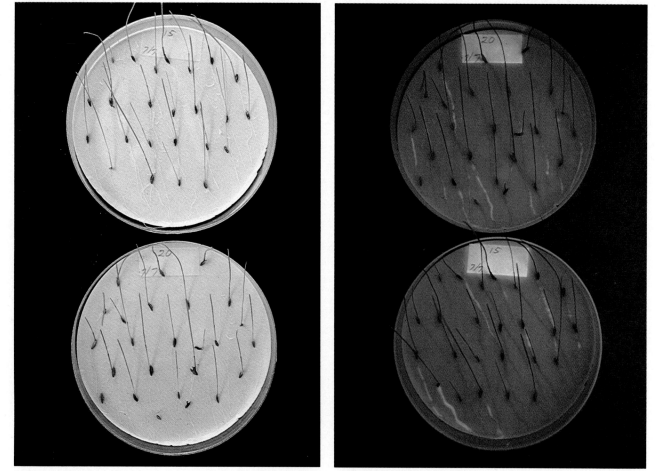

*Germinating a sample of improved ryegrass on filter paper (left) is a simple test of purity. If any of the germinating seeds show fluorescence when exposed to ultraviolet light, it confirms the presence of annual ryegrass (right).*

*Germination time sequence: Four different grasses are sown in identical soil mixes and lightly covered with a mulch. From left to right: 'Manhattan,' 'Merion,' 'Fortress,' and common bermudagrass.*

*'Manhattan' ryegrass was the first to germinate, followed closely by 'Fortress' fescue. Both the common bermudagrass and 'Merion' Kentucky bluegrass took between 13 and 14 days to emerge.*

*'Manhattan' and 'Fortress' showed faster growth rates compared to the bermuda and the bluegrass. The most rapid growth after germination of any type grass occurs if the soil is rich in nutrients and the time of year is most favorable.*

# The new lawn

**A beautiful new lawn can have a dramatic effect on a home or building. Landscape plantings are accentuated, and the strong lines of walls, driveways, and sidewalks are softened by an expanse of grass.**

With the goal of a lush, green lawn in mind, it is easy to hurry through the initial steps of establishment, but nothing could be more unfortunate. Your first decisions and procedures will be most important to the future of your lawn.

Answers to questions like "Which grass should I plant? . . Do I want to sow seed or use sod, sprigs, stolons or plugs? . . How will I water? . .", all should be fully thought out in advance of any labor. It's a good idea to look through this entire book before beginning work. A little forethought will save you a lot of future headaches.

## Ten steps toward a new lawn

We've seen many different ways of getting from bare ground to a new lawn. Some people simply spread seed over their existing ground without preparing the soil. Few lawns started this way succeed, or at the least reach their optimum appearance level. New techniques such as hydro-mulching are becoming increasingly popular. (See photo.) Regardless of the planting method, success is still measured by long term results.

Here we list the steps of site preparation that lead to a long lasting, beautiful lawn. Following a logical order of events prevents costly backtracking and repetition of similar steps.

1. **Test soil**
2. **Remove debris**
3. **Control persistent weeds**
4. **Rough grade the site**

◁

*The essence of freshness — new blades of grass, as yet unmowed, glisten with dew in the early morning light.*

5. **Add high phosphorus starter fertilizer and lime or sulfur (if necessary)**
6. **Add soil amendments or top soil, if needed**
7. **Cultivate thoroughly**
8. **Install underground irrigation**
9. **Final grade the site and settle excavation areas**
10. **Lightly roll**

## Soil sense

Much of the success of your lawn will depend on how you prepare the soil. It helps to remember that, unlike a vegetable garden where the soil can be rebuilt each year, grass roots utilize the same soil year after year. Although most nutrient deficiencies can be corrected after the lawn has been established, changing the soil structure under growing grass is difficult and expensive. The time and effort you put into preparing the growing medium will be reflected in the health and beauty of your lawn for years to come. This is true for lawns grown from seed as well as vegetative plantings such as sod. Even though sod has a little soil already attached, site preparation is still critical to success.

Gardeners describe soil types in many ways — heavy, light, clay, sandy, loamy, rich loam, poor soil, lean soil. Scientists and horticulturists classify soils by the proportion of sand, silt, and clay they contain. These designations are based on the size of the soil particles, clay being the smallest, silt bigger, and sand the largest. A soil's texture is determined by the blend of these various particles.

*Hydromulching is a new and different way to start a new lawn. Seed is mixed with a paper mulch and water, and sprayed through a hose onto the seed bed.*

For proper growth, plants need air in the soil, available moisture (but not standing water), and a supply of mineral nutrients. If soil has plenty of clay, holding on to nutrients is no problem, but the small clay particles that cling closely together hold water, and leave little room for air. Squeezed into a ball, clay soil clings together tightly; water penetration is slow. Drainage is the main problem in clay soils; the lack of which often results in suffocation of plant roots. You know you have a clay soil if it's rock hard when dry and gummy when wet.

Sandy soils have lots of room for air, but moisture and nutrients disappear quickly. Water sinks right into sandy soil without spreading, and dries up in just a few days after watering. When sandy soils are squeezed into a ball, they quickly fall apart when the ball is released.

In between a sandy or clay soil and the one best for plant growth, is a loam soil. It contains a combination of clay, silt, and sand which retains nutrients and water while still allowing sufficient room for air.

Chances are your soil is not the perfect loam, in which case it would benefit from the addition of organic matter. Even if it is an ideal soil, heavy foot traffic or perhaps construction activity around new homes can severely compact it, closing air spaces and restricting water and nutrient penetration. You've seen the effects of compaction in foot paths worn across a lawn.

## Improving soil texture

The best way to make either a heavy clay soil or a light sandy soil into a substitute for a rich loam is through the addition of organic matter — not just a little organic matter, but lots of it.

The addition of organic matter — compost, peat moss, manure, sawdust, shredded ground bark — makes clay soils more friable and easier to work. Organic matter opens up tight clay soils, improves drainage, and allows air to move more readily into the soil. In light sandy soils, organic matter holds moisture and nutrients in the root zone. The more organic matter you add to a sandy soil, the more you increase its moisture-holding capacity.

Enough organic matter should be added to physically change the structure of the soil to a depth of 6 to 8 inches — the area where most grass roots grow. The final soil mixture should be 30 percent organic matter by volume — about 2 inches of organic matter mixed into the top 6 inches of soil is usually sufficient.

A common problem for many homeowners is determining the total amount of organic matter needed to amend their entire lawn area. The chart on page 29 will assist in that calculation.

The type of organic material used depends a great deal on what is locally available. While decomposed barnyard manure and compost are very good, they often contain troublesome weed seeds. Peat moss is generally problem free and available, but also expensive.

Other types of organic materials commonly found in the North include buckwheat hulls, ground bark, apple or grape pomace, and composted leaves.

## The first step — testing the soil

The first step in preparing any soil for a future lawn is to have your soil tested. Many state universities test soils for a nominal fee. In other areas it may be necessary to go to a private soil testing laboratory.

In the chapter entitled "Lawns in your area" beginning on page 80, specific information on local soil conditions of the North are listed by states. Of the 25 northern states, all but Illinois provide soil tests through universities.

A soil test eliminates guessing the amounts of nutrients and lime to be added and often provides useful information on the soil's texture. Some give specific recommendations, others supply instructions on how to interpret results and take appropriate steps. If you have any unanswered questions, consult your County Extension Agent.

## How to take a soil test

First of all, obtain any necessary forms and questionnaires from your local Cooperative Extension Service office or private soil lab. Information supplied through these forms will assist the lab in making specific recommendations for your site. Typical questions are: "How large is the sample area? Has fertilizer or lime ever been added? To what degree is the land sloped?"

To collect the soil, you will need a clean non-metal bucket or container, a soil sampler, garden trowel or spade, pencil and paper, and a mailable container that will hold about a pint of soil.

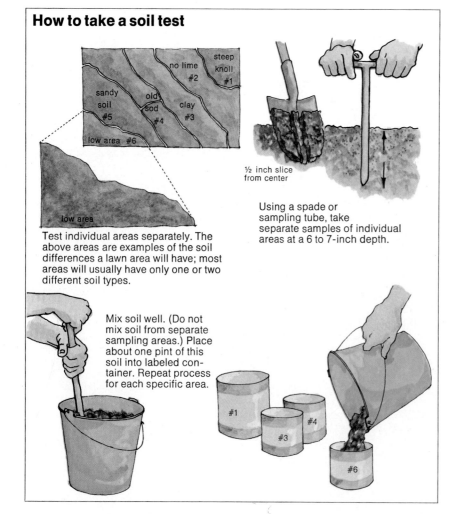

### How to take a soil test

Test individual areas separately. The above areas are examples of the soil differences a lawn area will have; most areas will usually have only one or two different soil types.

½ inch slice from center

Using a spade or sampling tube, take separate samples of individual areas at a 6 to 7-inch depth.

Mix soil well. (Do not mix soil from separate sampling areas.) Place about one pint of this soil into labeled container. Repeat process for each specific area.

To get reliable soil test results, you must take a representative sample. This means the soil should be gathered from 15 to 20 spots in any one sampling area. Low spots, trouble spots, and areas with obvious soil type differences should be treated as separate sampling areas.

Soil samples should be taken to a depth of 6 to 7 inches, ideally with a soil sampling tube. The hollow shaft of an old golf club or curtain rod will usually suffice. If you don't have a sampler, dig a V-shaped hole 6 to 7 inches deep with a spade or garden trowel. Remove a ½-inch slice from the smooth side. Soil samples from one sampling area should be mixed together thoroughly in the bucket. Allow to dry before proceeding.

Place about a pint of this soil in a sturdy carton or plastic bag, label it properly, and mail it to the soil lab. Record where each sample was taken. Also provide any additional information on the history of the land, if pertinent.

## Preparation of the planting site

The amount of work necessary to prepare the soil prior to seeding or sodding obviously depends on its present condition. If you are lucky enough to have a rich loam soil and a proper grade, little may need to be done beyond thorough tilling, fertilizing, and raking. Usually though, more work will be required.

To start with, clear all debris from the planting area. Rotting wood can cause low spots as it decomposes and can serve as a food source for termites. Stones and cement can damage tillers and other equipment.

It is also a good idea to determine the dimensions of your lawn area with a tape measure. Methods for figuring lawn dimensions are explained on page 96. These figures will be useful later in deciding how much amendments to add to the soil.

Next, establish a rough grade by filling low spots and leveling hills. On most lots there are fixed grade points such as house foundations, sidewalks, driveways, and trees. When grading, both rough and finished soil must be distributed so elevation changes between fixed points are gradual.

The ideal grade is a 1 to 2 percent slope away from the house to avoid water drainage toward the foundation. That's about a 1 to 2-foot drop per 100 feet. A long string and a level will be useful in determining the slope.

If the slope is not made to order, rough grading should be done before top soil or amendments are added. This will ensure good uniform soil to the depth of the root zone once the soil has been corrected. If the original soil is acceptable but the grade is wrong, the top 6 inches should be removed, the grade corrected, and the soil returned.

In areas where underlying hardpan or heavy clay soils prevent proper drainage, drain tiles may need to be installed. If this is the case, consult a competent drainage contractor for advice. Drainage work should be done after the rough grade has been established, but before top soil and amendments have been added for the final grade.

If soil is to be moved or placed around trees, take precautions not to disturb roots. Trees in the lawn deserve special care. For further advice, see the section, "Lawn tips," pages 92 to 93.

While working on the rough grade, you should also begin thinking of ways to make later lawn care easier. Header boards and mowing strips accent landscaping lines as well as help contain vigorous grass species.

Once the grade is sloped the way you want it, add the organic material so the final 6 to 8 inches of soil is about 30 percent organic matter. If top soil is replaced or added, spread half of it over the area and thoroughly till it in. This creates a transition zone between underlying soil and new soil. After you have done this, add the other half.

If you plan to install sod, keep in mind the final grade should be about one inch lower than the grade for a seeded lawn, so the sod will fit flush against sprinklers and sidewalks.

Next, add starter fertilizer (high phosphorous) and if the soil test indicates, lime or sulphur. Thoroughly till the soil.

It's important to carefully mix the top 6 to 8 inches of soil. Make several passes with the tiller in opposite directions to ensure soil, organic matter, and fertilizer are properly blended.

Once everything is mixed, it's time to install underground irrigation, if that is what you have decided upon. Waiting until all the tilling is finished will avoid potential damage to pipes.

(continued on page 32)

## Mulch coverage in cubic yards

| Sq. Ft. of Area | Thickness of mulch | | | | | | |
|---|---|---|---|---|---|---|---|
| | ⅛" | ¼" | ½" | 1" | 2" | 3" | 4" |
| 1,000' | .39 | .78 | 1.56 | 3.12 | 6.24 | 9.36 | 12.48 |
| 2,000' | .78 | 1.56 | 3.12 | 6.24 | 12.48 | 18.72 | 24.96 |
| 3,000' | 1.17 | 2.34 | 4.68 | 9.36 | 18.72 | 28.08 | 37.44 |
| 4,000' | 1.56 | 3.12 | 6.24 | 12.48 | 24.96 | 37.44 | 49.92 |
| 5,000' | 1.95 | 3.90 | 7.80 | 15.60 | 31.20 | 46.80 | 62.40 |
| 10,000' | 3.90 | 7.80 | 15.60 | 31.20 | 62.40 | 93.60 | 124.80 |
| 20,000' | 7.80 | 15.60 | 31.20 | 62.40 | 124.80 | 187.20 | 249.60 |
| 40,000' | 15.60 | 31.20 | 62.40 | 124.80 | 249.60 | 374.40 | 499.20 |

Three cubic feet will cover 36 square feet to a depth of one inch.
There are 27 cubic feet in a cubic yard.

## Approximate amounts of ground limestone needed to raise pH

| Change in pH desired | Pounds of ground limestone per 1,000 square feet* | | | | |
|---|---|---|---|---|---|
| | Sand | Sandy loam | Loam | Silt loam | Clay loam |
| 4.0 to 6.5 | 60 | 115 | 161 | 193 | 230 |
| 4.5 to 6.5 | 51 | 96 | 133 | 161 | 193 |
| 5.0 to 6.5 | 41 | 78 | 106 | 129 | 152 |
| 5.5 to 6.5 | 28 | 60 | 78 | 92 | 106 |
| 6.0 to 6.5 | 14 | 32 | 41 | 51 | 55 |

*In the southern and coastal states, reduce the application by approximately one-half.

## Approximate amounts of soil sulfur to lower pH

| Change in pH desired | Pounds of sulfur per 1,000 square feet | | |
|---|---|---|---|
| | Sand | Loam | Clay |
| 8.5 to 6.5 | 46 | 57 | 69 |
| 8.0 to 6.5 | 28 | 34 | 46 |
| 7.5 to 6.5 | 11 | 18 | 23 |
| 7.0 to 6.5 | 2 | 4 | 7 |

# Installing a seed lawn

### Carefully rake and level the seedbed **1**

Use a steel rake for final grading and removal of stones. In large areas, a piece of chain link fence or wooden drag can be especially helpful in leveling. Take your time on this step — it will prevent scalping from lawn mowers and water puddles from occurring later on. Correcting the grade after the lawn is established is difficult.

### Sow the seed **2**

Grass seed can be sown with the same equipment used to spread fertilizer if the spreaders are calibrated to distribute seed at recommended rates. As long as you don't drastically over or under seed, the results will be the same. Lawn seed can also be sown by hand.

Regardless of the seeding method, divide the seed into two equal lots. The second lot should be seeded at right angles to the first, covering the entire lawn area in each pass. When using wheeled spreaders it may be necessary to touch up edges by hand.

### Lightly rake the seed in and roll **3**

To ensure good contact between seed and soil lightly rake the entire area with a rake. Be sure not to rake the area too roughly, this can redistribute seed or ruin the final grade. Hard raking can also bury grass seed too deep. A depth of ⅛ inch to ¼ inch (depending on seed size) is usually considered good for seeding.

# 4 Add mulch

Mulching the area where grass seed has been sown will hasten germination by keeping soil moist, while also providing protection for young seedlings. On slopes, mulching can be useful in preventing soil erosion while watering.

Many materials can be used as mulches. Here, a thin layer of peat moss is applied with a peat applicator available at local rental yards. In areas that have abundant rainfall or strong winds, a heavier mulch is advisable. Although wind is often a problem with light-weight mulches, various types of netting are available to solve this problem.

The mulch covering should be thin enough to expose some of the soil of the seedbed. Never completely cover the area. If light mulches such as peat are used, follow it up with a rolling. Rollers are usually available on loan from nurseries, or at rental yards. Rollers should be one-fourth to one-half full of water to provide the necessary weight.

# 5 Water thoroughly

Improper watering probably causes more failures in a newly seeded lawn than any other one factor. For even germination, the very top layer of soil (always the first to dry out) must stay constantly moist. A thorough soaking is required after sowing and then as many as three to four light sprinklings by hand each day until the young grass is established. How long establishment takes depends on the variety of species of grass, the time it takes to germinate, its rate of growth, and daily weather. More frequent watering will be required if it is hot or windy.

Water with a fine spray or mist-type nozzle to minimize moving soil or washing seed away. Avoid standing water.

Stringing the area with brightly colored flags will warn neighbors and children, but not necessarily dogs, to stay off.

## Weed control

You will save yourself time and trouble later on if you take steps to eliminate weeds now. There are several methods; most will take at least a month to be effective, and safe.

Methyl bromide completely sterilizes the soil but is very dangerous and should only be used by professionals.

Metham, known under the trade name Vapam, is a useful pre-plant fumigant that requires 30 days to pass after treatment before you can seed.

## 30 days delay before seeding

If time is not a factor, you can keep the prepared seedbed wet, allowing weed seeds to germinate, and then kill them with a contact herbicide. Or, allow the soil to dry and lightly rake the surface to kill new seedlings as they emerge. Let the soil dry completely before watering again. If this is done three or four times, most of the weeds will be killed, leaving fewer weeds to compete with the grass seedlings.

Be sure to read the labels of all these chemicals carefully. Do not sow any seed until the chemicals have dissipated. Check to see if the soil is safe by planting some quick germinating seeds such as radishes. If they come up and begin normal growth, it's safe to sow seed or lay sod.

Be very careful around trees and shrubs. Many of these chemicals will kill them as well. Read the label!

## Final grading

Final grading should be done just prior to planting. The smooth bed can be ruined if it is left too long.

Take time raking and smoothing the area to be sure it is free of rocks and as level as possible. Correcting high and low spots later will be difficult. In large areas a chain or wooden drag can be helpful.

## Starting from seed

Regardless of the quick effect of sodding, certain pleasures are afforded to the person who chooses to start a new lawn from sprigs, stolons, or seed. Few colors are as bright yet as soft as young green grass. Growth occurs so quickly that the feeling of actually growing something is more intense; the part you play seems more important. The person who grows his own lawn feels "more the gardener."

To be sure that planting your lawn from seed is a pleasant experience, you should become familiar with lawn seed, how it is packaged, mixed, and the rates at which it is sown. Read about lawn seed on pages 20 to 25.

The time of year you seed is important. Cool-season grasses such as the bluegrasses and fescues, which are most common throughout the northern United States, are best sown from late summer to early fall. Allow four to six weeks before the first frost so the grass will be well established before the onset of cold weather.

## Starting with vegetative forms

In the most southernly or easternly transition zones of the North, many of the warm-season grasses will be available only in the vegetative forms of stolons, sprigs, plugs, or sod. Bermudagrass, St. Augustinegrass, and hybrid bermudagrass are available as sprigs. However, common bermuda and centipedegrass are often planted from seed. Sow warm-season grasses in late spring or early summer.

Cool-season grasses can be sown in spring and warm-season grasses in late summer, but planting at these times of the year send young grass right into weather less than ideal for active growth. Cool-season grasses may go dormant in warm weather, warm-season grasses go dormant when it turns cool. Weeds may not follow this schedule and can take over before your new lawn is established. Never sow in the heat of summer — watering at that time will become almost a full time job.

*With proper grass selection and care, attaining a beautiful lawn is not as difficult and time consuming as it may seem.*

# Watering

There are probably more questions asked about watering than any other aspect of lawn care, and rightly so. As it is for any plant, water is one of grass's most basic requirements. Without it, of course, your lawn would not survive.

Watering your lawn would be simple if there were set rules for every situation on exactly how much water to apply and how often, but there are too many variables. Your lawn's water requirements depend on several things: the type of soil you have, the climate of your area, temperatures, wind velocity, humidity, the frequency of rain, the type of turf being used, and maintenance practices.

Even with all these particulars, rules do seem to surface upon reading many lawn books and university extension bulletins. After you have watered your lawn for a while, your own experiences and conditions will lead to some of these apparent rules.

It's important to understand that a good lawn watering program is dependent upon you, the waterer. By getting to know your lawn through close observation and by understanding your local climate characteristics, you can begin to answer many of the important questions yourself.

## How often should a lawn be watered?

The answer to this question is simply, when it needs it. A lawn has to be watered when the soil begins to dry out, before the grass actually wilts. At that stage, areas of the lawn will begin to change color, picking up a blue-green or smoky tinge. An even more evident signal is a loss of resilience — footprints will make a long-lasting imprint instead of bouncing right back

Soil moisture testers and coring tubes are other ways to check for adequate moisture. There are two types of moisture testers — mechanical and electrical. The mechanical type, called a tensionmeter, has a porous tip and a water-filled tube. Water in the tube can be pulled out by dry soil. The suction created is measured on the gauge. Tensionmeters are left in place, once installed. The electrical type operates on the principle that wet soil conducts electricity better than dry soil. A coring tube takes a plug of your lawn and the underlying soil. It allows you to see and feel the moisture level of your lawn's soil.

How long your lawn can go between waterings depends on several things. Roots grow only where there is water. If you constantly wet the top few inches of soil, roots won't venture any deeper. Eventually, the limited size of the root system will force you into watering more often. That means trouble, because frequent watering keeps the surface wet, ideal for weeds and diseases. If roots go deep into the soil, they can draw on a larger water supply and the lawn can go much longer between waterings.

Soil conditions can also affect how often you need to water. For example, 12 inches of loam soil will hold about an inch and a half of water, a sandy soil about half that much, and a clay soil twice as much. Lawns in sandy soil will need water more often than those in a rich loam. Lawns in a clay soil will need water less often, and it will have to be applied at slower rates to avoid wasteful runoff.

Different types of grasses have different water requirements which also affect watering frequency. Grasses are listed according to their drought tolerance on page 19.

Local weather patterns are also important. Seasonal rain can play an integral part in a watering program. When it's hot and windy, it's obvious more frequent watering is required.

In areas of the Midwest and Northeast blessed with ample summer rain, watering may only need to be supplementary. Cool-season grasses like bluegrass or fescues usually go dormant in the hottest part of the summer, returning to full vigor in cooler fall weather. The New York State Extension Service has this to say about summer watering of cool-season grasses: "If your lawn will not survive an ordinary drought without watering, it probably needs rebuilding. You will avoid numerous problems and save money and effort if you can learn to accept brown turf in occasional dry summers."

Nonetheless, many people do want to keep their lawns green in summer, as shown by the increasing numbers of underground irrigation systems being installed. If you want to keep your cool-season grass green in summer and have started a watering program in the spring, continue throughout the summer. If the lawn does go dormant, let it stay that way. Too many fluctuations between dormancy and active growth can weaken a lawn.

Here are some watering rules in case of drought.

**1.** Do not apply fertilizer to lawns when drought conditions exist.

**2.** Mow your grass higher and less

*Here, sprays of sparkling water refresh more than the lawn.*

*In order to water efficiently, you need to know your sprinkler's pattern and rate of distribution. Evenly spaced containers on the lawn area show how much water falls in specific areas. In our test, the stationary fan type applied water unevenly.*

often. However, don't let it grow a third more than its recommended mowing height.

**3.** Reduce weed competition.

**4.** Irrigate without runoff to root zone depth (about 6 to 8 inches), and only when your lawn shows the need.

On pages 80 through 89 are local weather characteristics for northern climates. They should be helpful in setting up your specific watering program. Rain gauges are also useful. By knowing how much rain has fallen, you can tell how much supplemental water is needed. Don't be misled by light drizzles that supply very little moisture to the soil. However, watering right after a light shower may be an effective way of reducing water use.

## How much water does a lawn need?

To keep grass roots growing deeply, the soil should be moistened to a depth of about 6 to 8 inches. This should take between 1 and 2 inches of water over the lawn surface. Depending on the weather and the soil type, the average lawn will deplete this amount of water in about one week. To tell if the water has gone down that deep, wait 12 hours and check with a soil sampler. Or, simply poke a screw-

driver into the ground. If it penetrates about 6 inches without much resistance, the lawn is usually wet enough.

Water should be applied as uniformly as possible, and no faster than the soil can absorb it. Avoid applying so much at one time that it results in wasteful runoff. If this occurs, divide your watering into timed intervals. Sprinkle until the soil can't take anymore and stop for 20 or 30 minutes to allow for absorption. Continue until the desired amount has been applied.

## What time of day should the lawn be watered?

This question has been answered in many ways, not all of them correct. Some suggest that afternoon watering causes sun scald of the grass blades. This has proven to be false. Others suggest that moisture left on a lawn overnight from a late afternoon or evening watering promotes disease. In both cases, these statements, need to be qualified.

First of all, there are several disadvantages to afternoon watering. At that time, evaporation caused by the wind and sun are at a maximum. Also, less of the water applied is actually made available to the lawn. Wind can disrupt sprinkler patterns, causing poor coverage. Local water consump-

tion is usually highest in the afternoon which can result in low water pressure. Keep in mind, too, that drought symptoms are more evident in the afternoons and evenings. These symptoms can be induced by the higher temperatures and winds typical of that time of day, but are not always an indication of water stress. Often the grass will regain its color as temperatures and winds subside.

Whether or not afternoon or evening watering promotes disease is still under some debate among experts, but it shouldn't cause any uncertainty in your watering program. Most lawns become wet at night naturally by dew. Cultural practices such as proper fertilizing, regular dethatching, and mowing at recommended heights will do more to prevent disease than watering at times other than in the afternoon. If you feel a wet lawn at night is increasing disease problems, water in the early morning rather than evening. This will save water and your lawn will have less moisture at night.

Early morning, then, is an ideal time to water, but the answer to the question "when" still remains: *water when the lawn needs it.*

## Watering new lawns

There is a different set of rules for watering a newly seeded or sodded lawn. Sprinkling is, at the least, an everyday requirement. The germination of seed or the knitting of sod roots to new soil will often require watering more than once a day. We've discussed new lawn watering in detail on page 29.

## Portable sprinklers

As we said previously, you have to understand your lawn's requirements and signals. It is equally true you must be very familiar with your sprinkling equipment. Whether you choose a reliable, portable sprinkler, or an automatic, underground system, the rates at which the water is applied and the pattern of water distribution will vary. Automatic systems, if properly designed and installed, are usually more precise and predictable. If you do choose to water with portable sprinklers, look over the many types with a skeptical eye, and a thought for uniform coverage and minimum water waste.

There are many types of portable sprinklers, so consequently, there are many patterns of water distribution. Even individual sprinklers of the same type can have completely different patterns. Without knowing this, a very conscientious waterer can end up with over and under-watered sections of lawn. This produces uneven green and brown areas, and unnecessary weeds and disease. Along with knowledge of soil and climate conditions, sprinkler patterns and water distribution are very important aspects of watering.

## The container test

There is an easy way to measure sprinkler water distribution. Set up a gridlike pattern of small (same size) containers on a section of the lawn. The grid pattern may change for different types of sprinklers, but it's a good idea to start with a straight line of containers, extending them at set intervals, from close to the sprinkler head, to just outside the reach of the water. Turn the sprinkler on at the pressure you would normally operate for a set time and then record the amount of water deposited in each container. This will give you a good idea of the sprinkler pattern, as well as the amount of water distributed.

Realizing that a lawn needs about an inch or so of water per week, you can easily tell how long a sprinkler should be run and to what degree the pattern should be overlapped for efficient watering.

We bought 15 of the major types of sprinklers and measured their pat-

*Overlapping sprinkler patterns helps apply an even distribution. With overlapping, this whirling head sprinkler becomes efficient. Occasional hand watering assures even coverage.*

terns of water distribution using the testing method described previously It is important to repeat there can be variations between sprinklers of the same type, especially those made by different manufacturers. It is best to check your own sprinkler to be certain of its distribution and pattern.

The most inefficient sprinkler tested was the stationary fan type. Rates of water accumulating in the containers varied from 8 inches an hour in one spot, to 2 inches an hour just 4 feet away, to almost nothing very close to the sprinkler head. There was seemingly no predictable pattern that could lead to proper overlapping and efficient watering. However, to label the

fan-type sprinkler useless is unfair. As long as the water distribution is known, they can be valuable for spot watering or as a supplement to other types of sprinklers.

We also tested the popular oscillating-arm sprinkler. Many believe this sprinkler deposits maximum amounts of water near the sprinkler, the decreasing quantities towards the periphery as the arm moves farthest from vertical. We found this to be true of older models, but discovered a different story when we tested a newer model from a different manufacturer. The newer sprinkler stalls momentarily when the arm is farthest from vertical, thus depositing more water near

*Oscillating-arm sprinklers are designed to apply water over large areas, and are highly adjustable. Individual sprinklers differ; test yours to be certain of its pattern.*

the periphery of the pattern to even out the distribution. This demonstrates the need to test each individual sprinkler.

A third model tested was the whirling-head type. It deposited the largest amount of water close to the sprinkler and decreasing amounts at greater distances from the source of the spray. When this type of sprinkler is used without overlapping, water distribution is uneven. With a 50 percent overlap, its efficiency is increased and the sprinkler becomes quite useful.

Combining a little knowledge gained from experimentation and an observant eye, setting up a watering schedule with a portable sprinkler can be quite easy.

## Get to know your lawn

As you become more adept at observation, you will become the watering expert for your lawn. By paying attention to your lawn's signals, a regular watering schedule will unfold, but with you in charge, compensating for changes in weather and the passing of the seasons.

Certain areas of the lawn will consistently signal water need before others. It may be an area on a slight slope facing south with maximum sun that always dries out first. Or it may be an area exposed to more wind than others. These spots are clues, and will mark the time to begin watering. Hand watering isolated dry areas can sometimes extend waterings a day or two.

## Developing a water efficient lawn

There are other cultural practices besides watering deeply and less frequently that will increase your watering efficiency. Two major problems that result in poor water penetration are thatch and compacted soil. If bad enough, either one can actually repel water, causing wasteful runoff. Regular dethatching and aerification as described on pages 56 to 59, increase water penetration, provide air in the root zone, and aid in nutrient uptake.

Following recommended mowing heights or mowing even higher in hot summer months will also conserve water.

Proper fertilization is another important factor in efficient watering. Poor fertilization invites competition from water-hungry weeds, and reduces the wear-and-tear capacity of the lawn. On the other hand, over-fertilization promotes vigorous water-hungry growth of the lawn which can cause thatch to develop.

## About that hose

Most gardeners realize that a hose can be their best friend or their worst enemy. Improper use, or a hose of poor quality can do more harm than good. Does your hose have leaky connections? Is it impossible to roll it up? Is it long enough?

If you answered yes to any one of these questions, you probably need to make minor repairs or purchase a new hose. Repair is easy and inexpensive. On the other hand, although a high quality hose is more expensive, it will provide excellent service for a long time.

A well-made hose will be flexible in any weather. This is usually the case with high grade rubber and laminated filament hoses. It is seldom true of inexpensive plastic models. The hose you buy should be long enough to reach all areas of your yard, and have a large enough diameter to supply sufficient quantities of water. The larger the diameter of the hose, the more water it can deliver. Home garden variety hoses are available in ¾ inch, ⅝ inch and ½ inch diameters. The ⅝ inch is a usual choice for a medium-sized lawn area.

If your hose needs repair, there is a wide variety of hose repair equipment available, from clamp-on to screw-on kits. Our favorite is the brass screw-on type shown below.

If you have ever damaged plants when dragging the hose around, consider heavy wooden stakes in key areas of the garden.

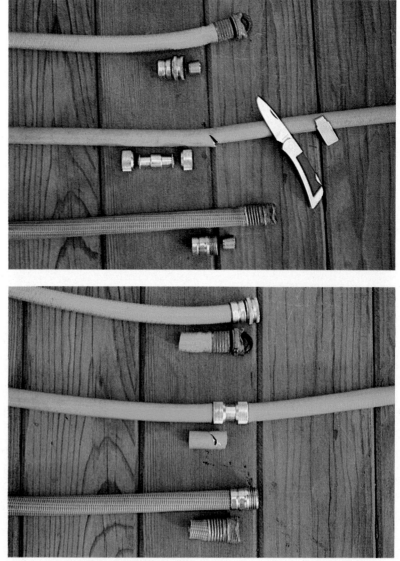

*Too many gardeners put up with broken or leaky hoses without realizing how easy and inexpensive they are to repair. The photo above shows some of the more common hose problems. Below, are the same hoses after being repaired.*

# Underground irrigation

The interest in underground irrigation systems seems to increase every year. The advantages over portable sprinklers are many, but the most obvious is the convenience of not having to constantly move sprinklers. In the majority of cases, they are also more efficient. Sprinkler heads apply predictable amounts of water over an exact area, eliminating the most objectional grievance of portable sprinklers — uneven water distribution. An underground system combined with an automatic timer can even water while you're away from home. It's important to stress that a poorly designed or poorly installed underground system will be just as bad or worse than a portable sprinkler.

The one disadvantage of an underground system is the initial cost of materials and the installation labor. But along with the increased interest in such systems, materials have become cheaper as well as easier to install. Galvanized steel and copper pipe have gradually given way to lightweight PVC (Poly Vinyl Chloride) plastic pipe and flexible polyethylene pipe. Heavy wrenches required to fit metal pieces together have been replaced by easy-to-use glue. Manufacturers have spent time and money in the production of simplified directions for home owners who wish to do the work themselves.

## Information for home installation

It is impossible in a book this size to give full, detailed information on how to install an underground irrigation system. Materials differ greatly between manufacturers, and there are too many variables for each specific site. What we have done is outline a typical underground installation. We've indicated where the problems might arise, how they can be solved, and the different types of equipment that can fit ideally into specific situations.

Choose the manufacturer as well as the supplier carefully. Consult neighbors who have underground systems, talk to irrigation specialists, nurserymen, or your County Extension Agent to get help in selecting a trade name that will best suit your needs. You can then either write the manufacturer, or obtain the available installation aids and catalogs from a local distributor.

## Installing a sprinkler system, step by step

### STEP 1
**Install valve system**
- ☐ Assemble valve assembly with PVC adapters in advance.
- ☐ Cut in tee for sprinkler main.
- ☐ Dig trench to valves.
- ☐ Install and flush valves.
- ☐ Check for leaks.

### Step 2
**Stake layout of system**
- ☐ Use stakes and string to mark sprinkler heads and pipe trench locations.

### Step 3
**Dig trenches**
- ☐ Use a flat-edged spade to dig v-shaped trenches (5″ wide at the top and 6-8″ deep).

### Step 4
**Assemble PVC pipe**
- ☐ Solvent-weld PVC pipe and fittings.
- ☐ Wait 12 hours.
- ☐ Insert plastic risers.
- ☐ Flush out pipe lines.
- ☐ Install sprinkler heads.

### STEP 5
**Test for coverage**
- ☐ Turn on each valve and be sure entire area is covered properly.
- ☐ Lower pop-up heads to proper level.

### STEP 6
**Backfill trenches**
- ☐ Fill trenches a little higher than the final soil line.
- ☐ Soak the soil to allow for settling.
- ☐ Check final leveling.

One thing to realize at the very start and its importance cannot be overemphasized, is the manufacturer of the system being installed will be your most helpful friend. Most will provide completely illustrated, easy-to-follow instructions that are useful not only to the individual who wants to do the entire job himself, but also to anyone who wishes to contract the job out to an irrigation specialist.

## Begin with a plan

After you've decided to put in an underground irrigation system, you need to decide how much (if any) of the work you are going to do yourself. Companies specializing in irrigation can often install a system within hours, and in no more than a few days. Do-it-yourself installation may take several weekends. If the sprinklers are to be installed prior to planting a new lawn, the clutter of equipment may mean nothing. In an established lawn it may be bothersome, or even damaging. Cost is also a consideration. If you are handy with tools and have the time, it is much cheaper to do it yourself.

However you decide, remember the importance of choosing reliable specialists to assist you.

Begin your sprinkler system with graph paper (10 grids to an inch is fine), a soft lead pencil, a dime store compass, and a measuring tape. A plan on paper will help you install a better system. Besides, a carefully prepared plan helps when ordering materials, makes it easier to get advice from your garden center, irriga-tion specialist, or hardware dealer, and serves as a record as to where the pipelines are laid.

Make your plan complete. A good plan is actually a bird's-eye view of your property drawn to scale, preferably 1 inch equaling 20 feet. With that scale, you should be able to fit all important details on a 8½ by 11-inch piece of paper. It should show all construction and landscape features which could affect the design and installation of the sprinkler system. This includes shrubs and trees, paved areas, fencing, and less apparent objects such as mailboxes, raised planters, and buried drainage or power lines. If significant, it is also helpful to note prevailing wind direction, sun and shade areas, steep slopes, as well as high and low spots in your landscape.

Draw the plan for both the front and back yards, even if you plan to install the system in only one area. You may want a similar system in another area at a later date. If you want to include sprinklers for trees and shrubs, indicate any water-sensitive or especially thirsty plants on the plan.

## An important number — gallons per minute

One of the most important aspects of building a successful sprinkler system is determining the available water in gallons per minute. This is usually abbreviated GPM. The best way to find available GPM is to use a gauge. A GPM gauge automatically compensates for friction loss, pipe corrosion, and similar variables. Most sprinkler suppliers will loan this gauge upon request.

It is possible to deduce available GPM without the use of this gauge. First, check the water meter size. It should be stamped on the meter itself. If it isn't, ask your local water company. Common meter sizes are ⅝ inch, ¾ inch, and 1 inch. Next, determine your static water pressure with a gauge measured in pounds per square inch (PSI). These gauges are much more commonly available than the GPM gauge. When figuring static pressure, use an outside faucet connected to the service line, and have all inside water turned off. Last, find out the size of the service line from your meter to the house.

## Types of pipe

Ease of handling, assembly, durability, flow characteristics, cost, and availability are reasons to recommend PVC pipe and solvent-welded fittings as the piping for sprinkler installations. Schedule 40 PVC is normally sold in 20-foot lengths. Use the heavy-duty schedule 40 for all pressure-holding lines. To save money and materials, use class 200 or class 315 pipe for all lateral lines that will never be required to hold constant pressure.

Flexible polyethylene pipe is also acceptable and very easy to use in sprinkler lines, but it cannot handle enough pressure to be used between the water meter and control valves.

The advantage of the flexible pipe is that you're not restricted to straight lines. Polypipe comes in 100-foot or 200-foot rolls and can be cut with a knife. Fittings are inserted into the pipe and held in place with stainless steel clamps tightened with a screwdriver or wrench.

## Sprinkler heads

While a wide variety of sprinkler heads are available for every conceivable application, most residential lawns and gardens can be best served by using adjustable, pop-up lawn sprinkler heads with full, half circle, and quarter circle watering patterns. When not in use, the head rests flush to the ground, out of the way of mower and foot traffic. It is important to remember that each sprinkler head is designed to discharge a specific number of gallons per minute (GPM) over a given radius, and that each head requires a certain water pressure in order to achieve its designed throw.

When adjusting the arc of a sprinkler head, check specifications to see that this does not drastically affect the rate at which the water is applied to the lawn (precipitation rate). This could change your watering strategy.

Square pattern and low precipitation rate heads are also available. Square patterns are useful in narrow areas such as side yards and parking strips. Use low precipitation heads in areas where runoff is a problem due

to a sloping grade or clay soil.

Besides pop-up spray heads, there are also impulse sprinklers which can be useful in large areas. However, these can be rather difficult to use efficiently in smaller lawns. In center areas of a lawn, especially if wind is a problem, consider pop-up sprinklers with rotary action, dispersing water in large drops rather than a spray.

## Drawing sprinklers on your plan

Set your compass to match the radius of the sprinkler heads according to the scale of your plan. Lightly draw in quarter circles wherever a 90° angle is shown within the area to be sprinkled. Next, draw the half-head circles normally located adjacent to paved areas, buildings, and property lines.

Finally, fill in center areas with full circle symbols. There are a variety of arcs available. Many installers have found one or more of these areas to be much more convenient for fitting a sprinkler spray to irregular shaped areas. Overspray can be a problem.

Here are a few good rules to follow.

**1.** Overlap the outer third of a sprinkler head's spray radius, more if wind is a problem.

**2.** Cut back the radius of your circles to accommodate design, but do not attempt to stretch it.

**3.** Design your system so that water is applied from the outside perimeter

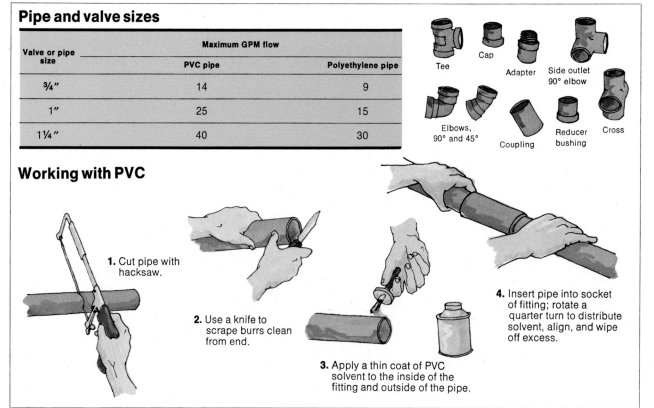

## Pipe and valve sizes

| Valve or pipe size | Maximum GPM flow | |
|---|---|---|
| | PVC pipe | Polyethylene pipe |
| ¾″ | 14 | 9 |
| 1″ | 25 | 15 |
| 1¼″ | 40 | 30 |

Tee

Cap

Adapter

Side outlet 90° elbow

Elbows, 90° and 45°

Coupling

Reducer bushing

Cross

## Working with PVC

**1.** Cut pipe with hacksaw.

**2.** Use a knife to scrape burrs clean from end.

**3.** Apply a thin coat of PVC solvent to the inside of the fitting and outside of the pipe.

**4.** Insert pipe into socket of fitting; rotate a quarter turn to distribute solvent, align, and wipe off excess.

inward toward the center.

**4.** Experiment with various full and part-circle head combinations and spacing patterns, until coverage is complete with no potential dry spots.

**5.** Water lawns and planted areas separately unless sprinkler heads are designed to deliver optimum amounts of water to the plants.

## Control valves

Your irrigation system will have to be divided into circuits which operate one at a time. There will probably not be enough available water pressure to water the entire lawn at once. Each circuit will have a separate control valve. Together all the control valves compose what's called the manifold, which should be placed in a convenient location, usually next to a doorway and out of reach of the sprinkler spray. One manifold each will be needed for both the front and back yard. Draw the manifold in your plan. Try to conceal the manifold with some sort of cover or box as the plumbing is seldom attractive. An anti-siphon valve will prevent backflow of water into the house supply. They are sometimes required by local ordinances and are always a good idea.

Use the three figures obtained earlier (water meter size, static water pressure, size of service line) to determine the gallons per minute available to any one circuit. Group the sprinklers into circuits, making sure the total GPM discharged does not exceed what you've just determined is available. It's all right to have less, but try to keep each circuit about the same. Do not mix different types of sprinkler heads (impulse, spray, shrub bubblers) in one circuit. Take your time planning your different circuits. It may take two or three tries to get it right.

Whenever possible, group sprinkler heads by the requirements of an area. In other words, water sloping areas

## Loss due to friction
## PVC pipe

(pressure drop p.s.i. per 100 ft. of pipe)

| Flow GPM | Pipe size | | | |
|---|---|---|---|---|
| | ½" | ¾" | 1" | 1¼" |
| 1 | .21 | .06 | .02 | |
| 2 | .76 | .22 | .06 | |
| 3 | 1.16 | .46 | .14 | .04 |
| 4 | 2.74 | .79 | .23 | .08 |
| 5 | 4.14 | 1.19 | .35 | .10 |
| 10 | | 4.29 | 1.27 | .37 |
| 15 | | | 2.68 | .78 |
| 20 | | | | 1.33 |

with low precipitation heads and windy areas with heads that apply larger drops of water.

## Valve and pipe size

Draw the piping in from the valves to the sprinklers. Avoid going under sidewalks and driveways if possible. Split the flow whenever you can so smaller-sized (cheaper) pipe can be used. Pipe size is determined from the maximum number of GPM that can flow through. Use the chart on page 38 to determine pipe and valve size. For example, if a circuit requires 16 GPM, available 1-inch PVC should be used. However, if the flow down the line is reduced to 8 GPM, the pipe size can be reduced to ¾ inch.

Pipe size from the control valve to the supply line should be the size of the largest valve in the system. If the distance between supply line and valves is over 100 feet, go one size larger.

## Pressure change due to friction or slope

Two factors can influence the water pressure available to operate a sprinkler head. One is friction — caused when water moves through the pipe. The other is a change in elevation between the water source and the sprinkler head.

Pressure loss due to friction is dependent on the length and size of the pipe and the amount of water traveling through. It is accumulative and can be determined in PSI per 100 feet of pipe. Increasing the pipe size will increase flow and decrease friction. (See chart.)

If your irrigation system runs up a slope, add almost half (.433 to be exact) a pound per square inch of pressure that you need for every foot of rise. If it runs down a slope, subtract this amount for every foot of fall.

## Check your plan

At this point you should be ready to begin installation of your underground irrigation system. In order to avoid costly problems, it is a good idea to have your plan checked by a specialist before you begin. The retail dealer who supplies your equipment may offer help, in which case you may have it checked free of charge. Otherwise, it will be money well-spent to engage the services of an independent installer.

## Installation

Installation specifics will vary between manufacturers. They should be

spelled out in detail in printed material available from dealers, distributors, or the manufacturer. The basic steps are outlined on page 37.

## Cold winter climates

In areas where the soil will freeze in winter, it is necessary to install drain valves at the lowest point in each circuit, as well as between the control valves and the first gate valve near the water meter. The latter will most likely be in the basement. Use a level to avoid any water pockets in the system.

The drain valves in each circuit should be aiming down on a slight tilt, covered with a short piece of pipe, surrounded with gravel and covered with visqueen plastic. Never put a drain valve in a fitting before the fitting is attached to the pipe; PVC solvent may clog the valve.

## Riser height and backfill

Before connecting the sprinkler heads, use a ruler to determine the proper length of the riser. This will depend on whether it's an old or new lawn, whether a new lawn is seed or sod, its eventual mowing height, and the height reached by the nozzle of a pop-up sprinkler. If the risers are too long, the sprinkler head may be damaged by mowers, and if too short, they may become clogged with soil. Make them longer if sod will be installed, shorter if you are starting a lawn from seed.

Several types of risers are available to make this easier. A cutaway riser has sections of thread in short increments along its entire length. Small ½-inch pieces are easily cut away one or two at a time until the proper height is reached. Flexible risers require proper height adjustment, but if by accident the sprinkler head is kicked or hit by a mower, they flex rather than break. Repairing underground damage to PVC can be troublesome.

Test your system first, then replace the soil in the trenches and water it thoroughly to settle it in. Repeat as necessary until the trenched area is level with the surrounding soil. This will avoid high and low spots.

## Automatic timers

For complete automation in lawn watering, you may want to install an electric timer and automatic valves on your system. Most manufacturers also supply timers.

Locate the timer where it can be protected from sun and rain and close to an electrical outlet; a garage is ideal. Its positioning may influence the location of your control valves.

# Sprigs, stolons, and plugs

With the exception of zoysiagrass (and in some areas along the eastern seaboard, bermudagrass), planting a lawn by sprigs, stolons, or plugs is limited to southern and southwestern parts of the United States, where warm-season grasses predominate. Because most of the warm-season grasses spread horizontally by above-ground stolons (referred to as runners from here on), or underground rhizomes, sections of the plants can be evenly spaced over an area. In time they will cover, forming a beautiful lawn. This planting method is not practiced with most cool-season grasses.

With some grasses, hybrid bermudagrass for example, planting vegetatively with sprigs, stolons, plugs, or sod is the only possible way because they do not produce viable seed.

The first step to any one of these three methods is to properly prepare the soil according to the instructions beginning on page 28.

## Sprigs and stolons

A sprig is an individual stem, or piece of grass stem. Regardless of what a sprig is technically, a rhizome or stolon, if it has at least one node or joint, it has the potential of developing into a grass plant and spreading. Sprigging is simply the planting of individual sprigs at spaced intervals. A suitable sprig should have roots or at least two to four nodes from which roots can develop. Bermuda, zoysia, and bentgrass are commonly planted by this method.

Sprigs can be bought by the bushel or obtained by buying sod and pulling it apart into separate sprigs. If bought by the bushel, they probably will be shipped to you from the point of origin in bags or boxes. Shipping usually takes place within 24 hours after shredding.

The soil should be ready to plant when they arrive. Keep the sprigs cool and moist until planting time, which should be as soon as possible. Only five minutes of sunlight can damage sprigs in plastic bags. Even when stored properly, sprigs will decay rapidly.

There are several ways to plant sprigs. One method is to cut 2 to 3-inch deep furrows in the seed bed, placing the sprigs in the furrows up to 12 inches apart (depending on how fast you want coverage). The furrows can be dug with a hoe and spaced from 4 to 12 inches; again, this depends on the rate of coverage you would like. Close spacing results in more rapid coverage, but naturally involves more material and labor.

If you use the furrow method, place the runners up against one side of the furrow so that any tufts of foliage are above ground, and the light-colored runner is below ground. Firm the soil around it and level the area as well as possible. A light rolling will help firm soil around runners and aid in the leveling.

It's best to begin working with slightly moist soil, but this often causes more problems than it's worth. In any case, *don't let the stolons dry out.* Water sections as you plant them, and keep the soil constantly moist until the runners are established.

Another method of planting sprigs is to place the runners on the soil at desired intervals and lightly press them in with a notched stick.

A third and faster method is called stolonizing, broadcast sprigging, or shredding. The sprigs are broadcast over the area like a mulch, either cut into the soil with a sprigging disc or covered with a mulch or soil and rolled. Peat moss, ground bark, or sawdust work well as mulches—about ¼ inch is satisfactory.

## Plugs

Plugging is exactly what it sounds like — small circles or squares of sod are plugged into the soil at regular intervals. Square plugs are cut from sod with a shovel or knife, while round plugs are cut with a special steel plugger similar to a bulb planter. The plugs are placed in corresponding size holes spaced 6 to 12 inches apart in the lawn area. The plugs are then tamped (or rolled) and watered. Although plugs do not dry out as fast as sprigs, keeping the surrounding soil moist is still very important. Coverage from plugs will be slower than sprigging, but less plant material is damaged or lost.

St. Augustine and centipedegrass are usually cut into plugs 3 to 4 inches in diameter and planted on one foot centers. Bermuda and zoysiagrass plugs are usually 2 inches in diameter and planted on 6 or 12 inch centers. Spacing determines the time it will take to achieve complete coverage.

When plugging or sprigging, it is usually necessary to top dress with soil or organic matter after the initial

## Planting methods for warm-season grasses

| Grass | Method |
| --- | --- |
| Bahiagrass | Seed |
| Bermuda-grass: | |
| Common | Sprigs, Plugs, Sod, Seed |
| All others | Sprigs, Plugs, Sod |
| Carpetgrass | Sprigs, Plugs, Sod, Seed |
| Centipede-grass | Sprigs, Plugs, Sod, Seed |
| St. Augustine-grass | Sprigs, Plugs, Sod |
| Zoysiagrass Z. japonica | Sprigs, Plugs, Sod |
| All others | Sprigs, Plugs, Sod |

A square yard of sod provides: 2,000 to 3,000 bermuda or zoysiagrass sprigs; 500 to 1,000 St. Augustine or centipede-grass sprigs; 324 two-inch plugs; 84 four-inch plugs; approximately one bushel of sprigs. Row planting requires about 2 to 6 bushels per 1,000 square feet. Broadcast planting requires anywhere from 3 to 10 bushels.

establishment to level the lawn. Irrigation and rain can cause the soil to wash out between sprigs or plugs, yielding an uneven and bumpy lawn.

The best time to plant plugs and sprigs and stolons is just prior to warming days of spring. The onset of warm weather will provide optimum growing conditions for warm-season grasses.

*Sprigs are individual grass stems or pieces of stems. Planted at regular intervals, they spread to become a lawn.*

# Sod lawns

Sod is turf that is grown commercially, cut into strips, and lifted intact with a thin layer of soil held together by the rhizomes, the roots, or netting. Installing a sod lawn is much like laying a carpet, with the objective of reestablishing the grass roots in well-prepared soil.

In the southern and southwestern United States and even coastal areas of the North, plugging or sprigging is the common way to install a lawn. Bermudagrass is available as sprigs, sod, or seed; St. Augustinegrass from stolons, 2-inch sod plugs, or sod; zoysiagrass from sprigs or 2-inch sod plugs, centipedegrass is available as seed, sprigs, or 2-inch sod plugs.

Compared with establishing a lawn by seed, sprigging, or plugging, laying sod yields much quicker results. A sod lawn can be functional in as little as two weeks, although some restraint should be used until its roots are properly knitted with the soil. This can be checked by lifting corners. Under proper conditions, sprigging of bermudagrass may cover in 8 to 10 weeks. Plugging of St. Augustinegrass can take 3 months to cover, and a seed lawn requires 14 to 21 days for germination, followed by a 6- to 10-week establishment period prior to use.

While timing of a seeded lawn is critical, a sod lawn, weather permitting, can be installed almost any time of year. Ideal times to put in sod are late summer and early fall for cool-season grasses, late spring and early summer for warm-season grasses. Cool-season lawns can also be installed in early spring.

Sod can also be installed in areas where a seed lawn may be difficult to establish due to traffic, or on a slope where erosion can be a problem.

The one drawback of sod is the initial cost and the labor involved, which can be substantial compared to a seed lawn. But what price tag can you place on instant results?

## Select a high quality sod

The first step is to select a high quality, healthy turf of a grass well adapted to your area and site.

Sod of cool-season grasses is generally available in the same varieties or blends of varieties that can be obtained in seed mixes. Mixtures usually include both shade-tolerant and sun-loving grass types.

Sod usually comes in rolled or folded strips from 6 to 9 feet long and two feet wide. It should be moist but not too wet, and definitely not too dry. If the sod delivered is high quality, it will be uniformly green. Don't buy any sod with poor color or yellowing.

The thickness of different varieties of sod may vary, but generally it should be about ¾ to 1 inch thick. If the sod is too thick, it will root slowly or poorly, too thin, and it will dry out too fast. It should not fall apart easily when handled.

Some states have a sod certification program to insure the sod is labeled correctly, and is relatively free of insects, weeds, and disease. If certified sod is not available, make sure the sod you buy originates from a reputable sod farm.

## Important — prepare the soil

Before the sod is delivered the soil should be thoroughly prepared according to the instructions on pages 27 and 28. Don't be fooled into thinking that because sod already has soil attached, that soil preparation is not important. It is just as important as it is with the establishment of a seeded lawn.

## After delivery

Sod is usually delivered on pallets to the site where it is to be installed. Once the sod arrives, it should be laid as soon as possible. Do not leave it rolled and stacked on pallets more than one day in hot weather. If it's cool, sod can remain rolled for 2 to 3 days. Store in a cool, shaded area. Be sure to keep the soil on outer pieces moist.

## Watering the new sod

Proper watering is the single most important step in the establishment of a sod lawn. Moisten the soil before laying sod. It's best to water a day or two in advance to avoid laying the sod on muddy soil. After the sod is in place, it may be necessary to water every day for up to two weeks until the roots have sufficiently knitted with the underlying soil. If a large area is being sodded it's better to work in sections. Lay the sod in one area, roll and water, then move on to another area. This is much less risky, especially if the weather is warm.

After watering, lift a corner of the sod to be sure the soil underneath is moist. An inch of water over the area is usually sufficient to wet soil and sod. Keep the soil moist at all times but not so wet that it is saturated.

The edges of the sod strips and borders along paths and driveways will be the first to dry out and the last to knit with the soil.

## Installing sod on a slope

When laying sod on a slope, start from the lowest point and move uphill. Always lay the sod so it runs perpendicular to the slope and stagger the joints to avoid excess erosion during irrigation or rain.

Pegging or staking sod strips may be desirable on steeper slopes. Three pegs 6 to 8 inches long will usually hold each sod piece in place. Place one peg near each corner and one in the center. Pegs should be driven through the sod vertically, not perpendicular to the slope, near the top edge of the strip.

## Mowing and aerification

The time of the first mowing will depend on the species planted. Newly turfed areas should be mowed as soon as the grass is 2½ to 3 inches high. It should be clipped frequently enough to prevent removal of more than one-third of the growth at one mowing. See pages 48 to 51 for further information on mowing.

Aerifying a newly laid sod lawn two or three months after installation will help in the formation of a strong, well rooted turf. Some lawn growers aerify even sooner. Moisture, air, and fertilizer can then pass through the turf more easily, into the root zone where they are needed.

*Where sod comes from: A cutting machine lifts strips of turf at a sod farm. Make sure the sod you buy is freshly harvested.*

# Installing a sod lawn

### Choose high quality sod 1

Many problems can be avoided if high quality sod of the proper type is purchased. Most states have sod inspection programs to insure that sod is free of weeds, diseases, and insects and that it is the variety or species it is advertised to be. Make sure sod originates from a reputable sod farm. Your County Extension Agent or local nurseryman should be helpful. In addition, many nurseries sell and install sod. See text for other characteristics of healthy sod.

### Prepare the soil 2

Because you are laying actively growing grass with good soil already attached, you may think it unnecessary to prepare the soil. Nothing could be more untrue.

Prepare the soil as you would for a seed lawn (see page 28), but make the final grade about an inch lower so sod will fit flush against sidewalks, driveways, and sprinklers. If the soil test indicates, add lime or sulphur.

Take time to make sure the soil is as level as possible, using a drag leveler if necessary. Once the sod is laid it is difficult to level. If large quantities of amendments have been added to parts or all of the future lawn area, wet the soil thoroughly to settle it, allow it to dry, and regrade.

### Spread fertilizer and moisten soil 3

If the proper amounts of fertilizer have been worked into the soil during site preparation, it is not usually necessary to fertilize again for 6 weeks or whenever the lawn starts showing the need. If fertilizer has not yet been added, rake in a high phosphorus fertilizer to a depth of 2 or 3 inches.

Sod should be laid on damp soil. Muddy soil causes footprints and uneven spots. Dry soil will lead to drying and eventual weakening of the sod. If the soil is dry, plan to wet it a day or so prior to delivery of the sod so it has adequate time to dry to a damp stage.

## 4 Keep sod moist

Everything should be ready for installation of the sod prior to its delivery. Sod should not remain rolled or stacked for more than one day in hot weather. In cooler weather it can remain healthy for up to two or three days.

Do not allow the soil on the outer rolls to dry out. Occasionally give the rolls a light sprinkling, but take care not to oversaturate them, or they will be difficult to handle.

## 5 Start with a straight edge

The easiest way to begin laying sod is to start with a straight edge, such as a sidewalk or driveway. If you have an irregularly shaped lawn, draw a straight line through it or string a line across it, and start laying sod to either side. Handle the sod carefully to avoid tearing.

The rolls of sod are heavy — each strip can weigh as much as 40 pounds. The truck pictured above is loaded to near its weight-carrying capacity. It's best to have two or three helpers ready to help as soon as the truck arrives.

On a hot day (like the day these photographs were taken) it is a good idea to lightly sprinkle the strips as soon as they are laid.

### Roll out 6 the sod

Place the loose end of the rolled sod tightly against the previously laid strip and carefully unroll it. Ends of sod pieces should be staggered much like a brick layer staggers the ends of the bricks.

Here's a good tip: when rolling out sod strips, stand or kneel on a board or piece of plywood to distribute your weight. Otherwise, you are likely to end up with pockets and uneven spots.

### Place edges 7 tightly together

To avoid unnecessary drying, keep the edges of the sod in as close contact as possible without overlapping. Firm the edges together with your fingers but do not try to stretch the sod.

If the gaps cannot be avoided, fill them with good soil or organic matter and pay close attention to them while watering; they will be the first areas to dry out. Do not attempt to fill small gaps (less than 3 or 4 inches square) with sod because these small pieces of grass usually dry out and die.

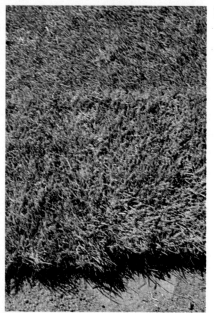

### Cut pieces to fit 8 with a knife

Along curved edges or unusually shaped areas, custom fit sod using a sharp knife or garden spade to cut the turf. As mentioned in Step 5, it is best to begin with a straight edge and work towards irregular areas.

## 9 Roll to insure good contact between sod and soil

After all the sod has been laid, roll it with a water-filled roller to ensure good contact between sod roots and underlying soil. It is best to roll perpendicular to the length of the strips. If the weather is warm, you may have to roll the sod in sections as it is laid.

Rolling will also have a leveling effect, but it is better to start with a level sod bed rather than compacting the soil with repeated rolling.

## 10 Water thoroughly

Improper watering after installation is probably the most common cause of failure in sod lawns. Once the sod has been rolled, water it thoroughly. The soil underneath should be wet to a depth of 6 to 8 inches. From then on, watch it closely. The edges of the sod and pieces along sidewalks and driveways will be the first to dry out, and the last to knit with the soil. They may require spot watering everyday, perhaps more often in hot weather. Make sure the underlying soil is always moist. Once the lawn begins to knit with the soil, you can begin to approach a normal watering schedule (see pages 34 to 39).

Avoid foot traffic, it can slow or damage the establishment of a sod lawn. If this is a problem, cordon the area with stakes, string, and bright flags.

# Lawn care

**This chapter is designed to simplify lawn care — from mowing and fertilizing to insect, weed, and disease control. Knowing how these aspects interrelate will help you learn how to take better care of your lawn.**

After all the what-to-do's and the what-not-to-do's have been outlined in this chapter, it is conceivable that a reader might become overwhelmed with the amount of work involved in caring for a lawn. This conclusion would be unfortunate, since lawn care is entirely up to the lawn owner.

We have presented the plan to grow the perfect lawn, but we also realize that the perfect lawn is not the goal of all people. We provide this information to answer the many questions concerning lawn care. We feel it is important to give you an understanding of how certain aspects of lawn care are interrelated, and how they affect a lawn's appearance.

## Level of maintenance

When it comes right down to it, any lawn looks better than having no lawn at all. Take a walk through your neighborhood and observe some of the lawns that look appealing. Notice at the same time how the lawn complements the house. Look closely; is it weed free? . . . are there bad spots? We doubt you'll find many perfect lawns, but lawns aren't required to be perfect, only to be appealing and functional.

The degree of lawn maintenance depends a good deal on convenience and the amount of time one has to spend on lawn care. *When* you fertilize, mow, or take care of weeds, probably depends on when you have the time. These tasks do not have to reduce the pleasure derived from caring for a lawn. Who can say who gets

◁

*It's worth it: Everything really does look better with a well-kept lawn.*

more enjoyment: the "lawn connoisseur" or the "Saturday morning mower"?

## Have a balanced program

Although the different aspects of taking care of a lawn can be broken down conveniently into chapters and subchapters, actual lawn care is not so precise. A lawn that is properly watered and fertilized will have fewer problems with weeds and disease. On the other hand, it will also have to be mowed more often. Regular mowing is a good method of weed control.

The key to success, no matter what your maintenance approach, is to have a balanced program of lawn care. If you mow less, water and fertilize less. If you enjoy getting outdoors and watering, balance this with extra fertilizing.

By understanding all of the needs of your lawn, you will be able to have the lawn you desire. More importantly, you will see that lawn care can be simplified and enjoyable.

*A little exercise on a sunny afternoon, the feel and fragrance of a fresh cut lawn — these are the pleasures of lawn care.*

# Mowing

Notwithstanding pages of magazine cartoons, it's our feeling that most people reading this book don't really mind mowing their lawns. Mowing is a good way to stretch muscles and get out among the neighbors. It's also difficult to imagine anything that smells or feels better than a freshly cut lawn.

Many people who want a handsome lawn don't realize just how important the job of mowing is. A lawn that is mowed when necessary and at the right height resists invasions of weeds, insects, and disease, and has a more lush, healthy look. Mowing infrequently, which often results in removal of too much grass at one time, will eventually produce a lawn with a thin, spotty, or burned out appearance.

## How often to mow

How often your lawn needs mowing depends primarily on three things: the kind of grass, how often and how much you water and fertilize, and of greatest importance, the time of year. The best rule of thumb is this: Mow when the grass grows to one-fourth to one-third taller than its recommended mowing height as shown in our chart. In other words, if your lawn's mowing height is 2 inches, mow when it's about 3 inches high, thus removing one-third of the height of the grass blade. Of course, this may not fit your natural, once-a-week habit or allow for vacations. In some cases, it means frequent mowing. For instance, well-fertilized improved bermudagrass in mid-summer may need mowing every two or three days.

The penalty for not following the rule is a stiff one. By letting grass grow too high and then cutting away half or more at once, you expose stems that have been shaded and are not adapted to strong sunlight. Grass leaves may be burned by the sun and turn brown. Mowing too high results in deterioration of green leaf tissue at lower levels. More importantly, roots are severely shocked by a heavy mowing and may need several weeks to recover. Research has shown a direct relationship between height of cut and depth of roots. Roots of grasses properly mowed at correct heights will grow deeper. Deep roots are an important advantage and make lawn care many times easier.

## Basically there are two types of mowers... but with several variations

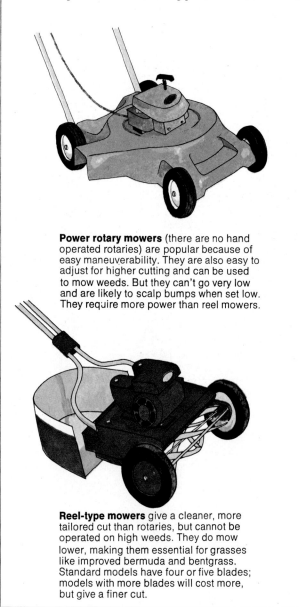

**Power rotary mowers** (there are no hand operated rotaries) are popular because of easy maneuverability. They are also easy to adjust for higher cutting and can be used to mow weeds. But they can't go very low and are likely to scalp bumps when set low. They require more power than reel mowers.

**Reel-type mowers** give a cleaner, more tailored cut than rotaries, but cannot be operated on high weeds. They do mow lower, making them essential for grasses like improved bermuda and bentgrass. Standard models have four or five blades; models with more blades will cost more, but give a finer cut.

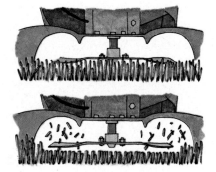

Rotary mowers cut like a spinning scythe. They stand rougher use than reel types. The blades are easy to sharpen, but if they get out of balance the whole mower shakes.

Reel mowers cut with a scissorlike action of spinning blades against a bed knife. They are available in rear and front throw models. Keep the blades sharp —have it done at a mower shop.

The time of year has a large effect on the frequency of mowing. The cool-season grasses of the northern states slow down or become dormant in hot summer weather. Mowing at this time will be infrequent — once every two or three weeks. During the cool months of spring and fall, most lawns will be growing at a maximum rate and require mowing at least every week.

How much water and fertilizer you apply affects the growth rate of lawns, and consequently, the frequency of mowing. Obviously, lawns maintained at high levels of growth-stimulating fertilizer will require more frequent mowing. For example, golf course greens are usually mowed several times per week, sometimes daily. More labor is one price of the luxurious lawn.

## The right height

The proper mowing height depends primarily on the kind of grass. Check the chart on page 51 for the recommended mowing heights of the major lawn grasses. First though, a little theory.

Generally, grasses grow either horizontally or upright. For instance, bermuda and bentgrass spread widely with lateral growing stems called stolons. These stolons parallel the ground as well as the cut of the mower, so are not normally mowed off. Unless grasses like these are kept mowed low, preferably with a heavy reel-type mower, they will in time build-up prodigious amounts of thatch.

Think of it this way. "X" amount of leaf surface is necessary to keep the grass plant healthy and growing. If that leaf surface is spread out low, over a wide area, the lawn can be mowed close to the ground without reducing the necessary leaf surface.

Vertically growing grasses cannot be mowed excessively low since the leaf surface area isn't enough to support the plant. Tall fescue, St. Augustine, bahia, and common Kentucky bluegrass fit into this category. Below a certain height (1½ or 2 inches from the ground), too little leaf surface remains to maintain a good turf.

Mowing too low probably ruins more Kentucky bluegrass lawns than any other practice. This is especially true in transitional areas where adaptation is marginal. Cut high, Kentucky bluegrass is much more disease resistant and can successfully compete

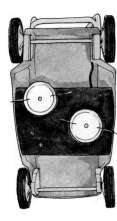

**Electric nylon mowers** cut grass with nearly the same efficiency as steel-bladed mowers, and are of course much more safe. Two counter-rotating discs powered by separate electric motors spin monofilament line to mow and trim.

**Push reel mowers** were *the* mower years ago, and are still quite useful for small lawns. They are less expensive and quieter than power mowers, and will cut efficiently when properly oiled and sharpened. The main difference between push and power mowers is that you provide the power.

**Riding mowers** and gang mowers (above) are best for lawn areas that are simply too large or time consuming to mow with a conventional reel or rotary. Gang mowers are often used to cut grass at parks and golf course fairways.

with weeds and insects. The tall growth also shades the soil, keeping temperatures lower for cool-loving roots.

Exceptions are some of the new varieties of bluegrass, which are essentially dwarfs. They are more compact and have more leaf surface in less area (see page 16). 'Fylking' and 'Nugget' are two varieties in this category. These dwarfs will tolerate much lower mowing (as low as ¾ inch) than common Kentucky bluegrass.

The best practice is to increase the height of cut as temperatures increase in summer and reduce it as temperatures drop. For instance, a tall fescue lawn should be cut 2 to 3 inches in early spring but allowed to grow 3 to 4 inches in the hottest months of summer.

Where shade is a problem, mow another ½ inch higher. This increases the light-trapping power for photosynthesis of the lawn.

## The clippings removal question

Some experts say clippings should always be removed, others say it's not necessary. Here's the way the facts sorted out for us.

Latest research has shown that clippings of cool-season grasses left on the lawn do not cause or contribute to thatch. It's the woody, slow-to-decompose stems, rhizomes, and stolons below the grass blades that contribute most to thatch buildup. Clippings of the warm-season zoysia-grass contribute to thatch build-up because they are more stiff and slow to breakdown. How much the clippings of other warm-season grasses contribute to thatch is still an open question.

Clippings return nutrients to the lawn. It's difficult to measure, but some estimates suggest that as much as one-third of a lawn's nitrogen requirement can be supplied by decaying grass clippings.

There are two reasons not to leave clippings on your lawn. First of all, they can be unsightly. Clippings are removed from many a high quality, intensely maintained lawn for just this reason. Secondly, if your lawn is not mowed frequently enough, too much grass will be cut off at one time. Instead of sifting down and decomposing, the clippings can mat on top and suffocate the grass underneath.

At the time of year when your lawn is growing vigorously, clippings will probably have to be removed. With very large lawns, removal of clippings becomes impractical, as is the case with parks and golf courses.

## Mowing new lawns

Newly seeded lawns are more delicate than established ones. That's why you have to be more careful mowing them. The soil is very soft and the grass plants usually aren't deeply rooted by the time of the first mowing. On the other hand, mowing young lawns, especially those planted vegetatively, encourages spreading, thus promoting a thicker lawn. Basically, use common sense and apply the same principles of proper mowing of any lawn.

You'll probably want to let the new grass grow a little beyond the normal recommended cutting height. Even then, mow it very lightly, removing less than a third of the total height.

If you can, use a mower that's not too heavy, especially if the soil is still soft. A lightweight rotary or a sharp push-reel mower is your best bet.

If the soil remains too soft or if the new grass is too loosely knit to mow without damage, wait. Let the lawn continue to grow, and then cut it gradually until it is down to the proper height (½ to ¾ inch reduction every second mowing until height is reached).

## Lawn mowing miscellany

✓Don't cut wet grass. Why? It can cause uneven mowing, the clippings are messy, and they can mat and suffocate the grass.

✓Pick up stones and sticks before mowing.

✓Alternate mowing patterns. Mowing the same direction every time tends to compact the soil and causes wear patterns.

✓For an attractive "checkered" finish to a lawn, mow it twice, traveling in opposite directions.

✓Reel mowers sometimes cause a ribbed pattern leaving the lawn with a washboard look. This is caused by a mower moving forward too fast for the height of cut. In other words, it's possible to push a mower faster than the blades can make regular cuts.

✓Check blade height with a ruler extended from the cutting edge to a flat surface such as a sidewalk or driveway.

✓Sharp turns with a mower can cause uneven cutting. Make wide turns or use sidewalks and driveways, but be aware of rocks or debris on pavement areas.

✓If the ground is uneven from settling of the soil in some areas, scalping may result as you go over the high spots.

✓Reel mowers are preferred for fine lawns. They cut the grass cleanly, with a scissorlike action and smoothly follow surface contours. They perform

*Riding mowers are expensive compared to other mower types, but they can be worth the cost if your lawn area is large.*

poorly on tall grasses and lawns with high, wiry seed heads.

✓The blades of rotary mowers are easy to sharpen at home. Only a small portion at the end of the blade actually cuts the grass. Sharpen the edge with a file or grindstone, making sure to even out any rough spots. Check balance before remounting.

✓Flail (also known as hammer knife) and sickle bar are less common types of mowers. Flail mowers use floppy, T-shaped blades revolving on a horizontal shaft to cut grass. They are useful in maintaining rough areas such as vacant lots and the sides of highways. Sickle bar mowers are used for cutting very high grass and weeds. It's the same sort of mower that farmers use to cut field oats and other hays and grains.

✓Experts disagree about the safest way to mow steep inclines. Some say across, others say up and down the slope. Use common sense, and be aware of the danger a power mower represents. Check its stability and be aware that a slipping mower can injure both you and your lawn. Perhaps the best way to handle a slope is to plant a ground cover that doesn't need mowing.

✓Trees in a lawn require special protection from mower damage. See pages 92 and 93.

## Lawn mowers

Almost every suburban homeowner has a lawn mower. The number of varieties and styles available proliferates each year. It pays to shop around to see what is available, to find the mower that fits your needs.

The two most common basic mowers are the reel and the rotary. Within each basic type are variations of gas or electric power, walking or riding, push, or self-propelled. Some have bagging attachments, or catchers.

Before buying a lawn mower, look it over carefully. Consider its maneuverability. Make sure the grass catcher is easy to take on and off. Check to see how easy the blades are to adjust. Ask about the safety features. These points will help you choose the right mower.

Mowers can be very specialized. Some are designed to cut high weeds, others are engineered to produce the carpetlike nap of a putting green. There are also the unusual types, such as the one that rides on a cushion of air, and another that cuts with spinning monofilament line.

**Reel or rotary:** The choice for most people is usually either a rotary mower or a reel. The rotary is by far the most popular. It is generally lower priced, more versatile, and easier to handle and maintain than the reel type.

However, rotary mowers require greater caution in use. They need larger motors with more horsepower, they can never cut as cleanly as a sharp, properly adjusted reel, and few can mow lower than 1 inch.

Reel mowers are available in manual (push) models, or powered with gasoline or electric engines. They cut with a scissor action, which produces the cleanest cut. They conform better to land contours than rotaries, but are impractical on rough, uneven ground or tall-growing grass. They can be adjusted to cut very low, so are the preferred type mower to use for lawns of bermuda or bentgrass, for example.

Power reel mowers discharge clippings from the rear or the front (rear-throw, front-throw). The rear-throw type is widely available and somewhat less expensive. It was most popular before the rotary became the common choice.

Front-throw reel mowers are used primarily by professional landscape gardeners. They are usually well made and can stand contant use. The weight and power of these mowers makes them perfect for the low mowing requirements of tough bermuda or zoysiagrass lawns. Height is also easier to adjust, usually with just a lever. Some can be adjusted low enough to cut right at the soil line.

**Riding mowers:** You will probably need a riding mower if your lawn is measured in units or multiples of acres. Be aware they are not toys — don't let children play with them. But they are somewhat fun to drive.

Riding mowers cut with the same action as their smaller counterparts — both rotary and reel. Rotaries are the most common.

## Mower maintenance

Proper care of your lawn mower will lengthen its lifetime as well as eliminate many time-consuming problems. The manufacturer's maintenance manual for your mower is the best guide. Basically, keep the blades sharp (this is very important) and be sure the motor oil is at the proper level. Clean the mower after use with a soft spray of water. Forceful clean-

## Mowing heights

| Grass | (inches) Height |
|---|---|
| Bahiagrass | 2-3 |
| Bentgrass | ¼ -1 |
| Bermudagrass | |
| Common | ½ -1½ |
| Hybrid | ½ -1 |
| Bluegrass | |
| Common | 2-3 |
| Improved (varies by variety) | ¾ -2½ |
| Buffalograss | 1-3 |
| Carpetgrass | 1-2 |
| Centipedegrass | 1-2 |
| Dichondra | ½ -1½ |
| Fescue | |
| Chewing | 1-2 |
| Red | 2-3 |
| Tall | 3-4 |
| Annual ryegrass | 1½ -2 |
| Perennial ryegrass | 1-2½ |
| St. Augustinegrass | 1-2½ |
| Zoysiagrass | ½ -1½ |

ing with water or air can push dirt into delicate bearings. Do not spray water onto a hot engine.

Keep gaskets and fittings tight; oil or gas dripping onto the lawn will kill the grass.

If you're storing the mower for winter, clean it and drain the gas tank. Come spring, change the oil, clean the spark plug, and refill the gas tank.

## Safety tips

Power lawn mowing equipment is so common it is taken for granted. But power mowers alone are responsible for thousands of accidents yearly. Follow the guidelines below and those of the mower manufacturer, and you'll miss becoming an injury statistic.

Don't disconnect manufacturer's safety features and always keep in mind the possible dangers.

Many fingers have been lost unclogging discharge chutes of rotary mowers. Make a habit of turning off the power and disconnecting the spark plug before thinking about reaching into the clogged grass.

Don't try to mow where the terrain is too steep or uneven. Again, many accidents have occurred on slippery, steep slopes.

Walk over a lawn area before mowing and look for rocks, toys, sprinkler heads, and other possible obstructions.

Don't allow children to mow until they are strong and mature enough to handle the job.

# The why, how, and when of fertilization

Lawn owners accept the fact that they must mow and water to be able to maintain their lawn's health. Some may question the need for fertilizer, but they shouldn't.

Lawngrasses live in what is basically an unnatural environment. They are crowded together and compete with each other, as well as neighboring trees and shrubs, for water and nutrients. They are mowed regularly and their clippings often removed.

Because of this competition and the unnatural demands placed on lawns, they must be fertilized. Just as a balanced diet works best for people and animals, the same is true of lawns — they need fertilizer for sustenance. Properly fertilized, the lawn will maintain good color, density, and vigor and will not easily succumb to insects, weeds, or diseases. Underfertilized, the lawn is not only less attractive, but is considerably more susceptible to environmental stress and damage.

## The nutrients a lawn needs

Scientists have singled out 16 different mineral elements as essential to the growth of all plants. Some are very common, such as oxygen from air and hydrogen from water. Others, such as zinc or boron, are needed in only minute amounts usually found naturally in most soils.

**Nitrogen** is by far the most important element needed by a lawn. It promotes rapid growth and gives lawns a healthy color. It is also the one most often in short supply. Watering flushes it from the soil and the growing plant needs a plentiful and continuous supply. Without sufficient nitrogen, growth stops and the lawn becomes pale and yellowish.

**Phosphorus** is the next most important element needed for healthy growth of lawn grasses. It is required to produce strong root growth. Phosphorus stimulates early root formation, particularly essential to the proper development of new plantings. It is not readily flushed from the soil by watering and is needed by grass in small quantities, so most balanced lawn fertilizers contain only a low percentage.

**Potassium** is the third element of critical importance. Like nitrogen, it is flushed out by water but at a much slower rate. It is very important to the hardiness and disease resistance of lawn grasses, and helps promote wearability. Potassium is needed in about the same quantity as nitrogen but soil minerals supply a considerable amount, therefore, not as much is added to fertilizers.

**Calcium, sulfur and magnesium** are also needed in relatively large amounts. Calcium is either present in adequate quantities in the soil or is added through periodic applications of lime. Dolomite (or dolomitic limestone) supplies magnesium as well as calcium. Most sulfur reaches a lawn through the air, water, or organic matter.

**Micronutrients** are elements needed in small amounts. If your lawn does not green-up with an application of nitrogen, the problem may be a shortage of iron. This is particularly true in areas where soil pH is high. (Yellowing can also be caused from sulfur deficiency, over-watering, manganese deficiency in sandy soils, and a pH less than 5.) A soil test may help solve persistent, seemingly soil-related problems such as these.

## Types of fertilizers

A little garden store shopping will reveal an abundance of lawn fertilizers. You'll see labels proclaiming "fast-acting," "slow-release," "organic" and so on. But if they all contain the same basic minerals, which they do, what's the difference? Here is a description of these products.

**Organic.** A chemist might argue that some man-made fertilizers are technically "organic." Here organic refers to a fertilizer derived from plant or animal waste.

The variety of organic fertilizers is endless. There are manures of all kinds — municipal sewage sludge, blood meals, and seed meals. They all share some advantages and some disadvantages. In some areas, they may be inexpensive and easy to obtain, yet the reverse is often true. Most have distinctly beneficial soil building properties covered in more detail on pages 27 to 31.

Usually the action of organics is slow, making it difficult to make a mistake and overfertilize. This is the major difference of organic fertilizers compared to synthetic fertilizers — nutrients are slowly released. (Bloodmeal is an exception. It is a fast release organic, almost as fast as mineral fertilizers.)

Organics are bulkier, heavier, and more difficult to handle. They have a low percentage of nitrogen so it is necessary to apply a much greater quantity at one time. (They may also be unpleasant to the nose.)

The main disadvantage of organic fertilizers is that the timing of nutrient release is not predictable. This is because soil microbes must be actively digesting the material making the nutrients it contains available to the lawn. Because microbes are most active when the soil is warmest, much of the organic carrier's nutrient is made available during warm weather which, as stated elsewhere, is not the best time for a lawn to receive a heavy fertilization.

**Soluble synthetic:** These are the most common fertilizers used on lawns today. They too have advantages and disadvantages.

The big advantage of this type of fertilizer is predictability. Because their characteristics are known precisely, you know exactly the effect they will have on the lawn. For many types of lawns this is an important feature. They are available to the lawn before the soil has thoroughly warmed in summer, they are lower in cost than organic fertilizers, and easier to handle. Less material need be applied since the percentage of nitrogen is usually high.

There may be more work required of the gardener who uses these. More applications are necessary because the effects are short term. If your lawn requires 8 pounds of actual nitrogen a year, almost that many separate applications will be necessary.

Further, there is the possibility of "fertilizer burn" if overapplied, if the lawn is wet as you spread the fertilizer, or if the fertilizer is not thoroughly watered in after application.

The exceptions are some "weed and feed" products which are formulated with soluble fertilizers and are designed for use on wet grass (when temperatures are moderate — under 85°.

**Slow release:** To some extent these fertilizers combine the characteristics of the organics and soluble synthetics. Usually they have a high percentage of nitrogen so handling large quantities of material is not necessary. But the possibility of fertilizer burn is highly reduced since the nitrogen does not become available to the plant all at once.

There are a variety of types, but most are categorized on a fertilizer bag under the heading "W.I.N.," meaning water insoluble nitrogen. Many of the commonly available lawn fertilizers are actually a combination of soluble nitrogen and W.I.N. nitrogen.

Slow release fertilizers are favored by many lawn growers because they make heavier applications of nitrogen possible, hence fewer applications are necessary. However, they don't provide a quick green-up. You will not have the degree of control of greening response that's possible with soluble synthetics, but will have slightly more than with organics.

## Percentage W.I.N.

In order to determine the actual percentage of water insoluble nitrogen (W.I.N.), it's necessary to do a little arithmetic. For example, if you have a 25-3-7 fertilizer with 7.6% W.I.N., multiply the 7.6 by 100 equalling 760. Divide the 760 by the total percentage nitrogen shown on the bag. In this case 760 divided by 25 equals 30.4 Thus 30.4% of the nitrogen is W.I.N.

Lawn experts have determined that fertilizers less than 15% W.I.N. are basically fast acting. Between 15 and 30% is medium and any more than 30% insoluble is a slow release fertilizer. A slow-release fertilizer is less likely to burn the lawn after application and is less subject to being flushed from the soil by water.

## Use a complete fertilizer

A complete fertilizer is one that contains all three of the primary nutrients: nitrogen, phosphate, and potash. Every state requires that the percentages of these three elements be prominently displayed on every bag of fertilizer. Always, the first number is nitrogen, the second phoshate, and the third potassium. An example is 24-4-8. These numbers state the percentages of nutrients in the bag compared to the total contents of the bag.

As a general guide, a 3 to 1 to 2 ratio of nutrients has proven to be good for home lawn fertilization. However, factors such as local climate,

soil conditions, and the form of nitrogen in the fertilizer can influence what's best in various localities.

A 3 to 1 to 2 fertilizer could have a formula of 21-7-14. It is not critical for a fertilizer to be exactly this ratio, but something close to it is recommended. For instance, a higher nitrogen ratio of 6 to 1 to 2 (formula 24-4-8) is common.

Generally this ratio of nutrients is properly applied by using the products of a lawn food manufacturer in a label-directed way. There are general purpose types as well as those designed for specific grasses.

These ratios are based on the demand of the growing lawn for these nutrients. Usually a lawn needs three to five times as much nitrogen as phosphorus and two times as much potassium as phosphorus. (Although nitrogen and potassium are needed by the plant in similar amounts, some nitrogen is flushed from the soil by water and is lost.)

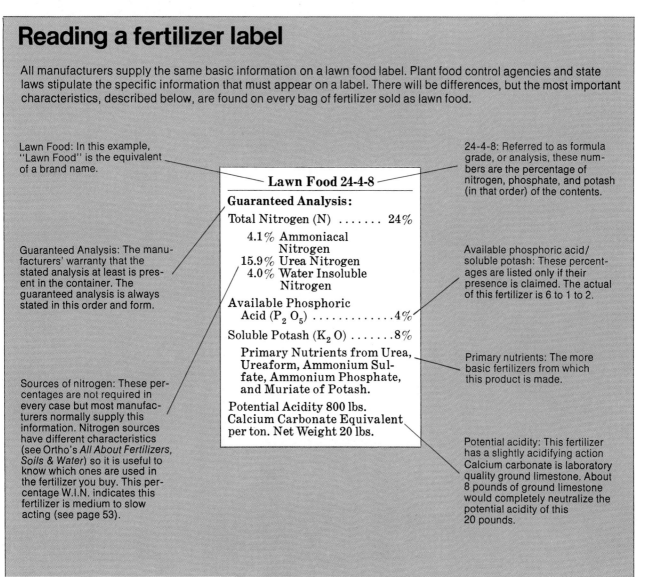

# Reading a fertilizer label

All manufacturers supply the same basic information on a lawn food label. Plant food control agencies and state laws stipulate the specific information that must appear on a label. There will be differences, but the most important characteristics, described below, are found on every bag of fertilizer sold as lawn food.

Lawn Food: In this example, "Lawn Food" is the equivalent of a brand name.

Guaranteed Analysis: The manufacturers' warranty that the stated analysis at least is present in the container. The guaranteed analysis is always stated in this order and form.

Sources of nitrogen: These percentages are not required in every case but most manufacturers normally supply this information. Nitrogen sources have different characteristics (see Ortho's All About Fertilizers, Soils & Water) so it is useful to know which ones are used in the fertilizer you buy. This percentage W.I.N. indicates this fertilizer is medium to slow acting (see page 53).

24-4-8: Referred to as formula grade, or analysis, these numbers are the percentage of nitrogen, phosphate, and potash (in that order) of the contents.

Available phosphoric acid/soluble potash: These percentages are listed only if their presence is claimed. The actual of this fertilizer is 6 to 1 to 2.

Primary nutrients: The more basic fertilizers from which this product is made.

Potential acidity: This fertilizer has a slightly acidifying action Calcium carbonate is laboratory quality ground limestone. About 8 pounds of ground limestone would completely neutralize the potential acidity of this 20 pounds.

### Lawn Food 24-4-8

**Guaranteed Analysis:**

Total Nitrogen (N) ....... 24%

    4.1% Ammoniacal Nitrogen
    15.9% Urea Nitrogen
    4.0% Water Insoluble Nitrogen

Available Phosphoric Acid ($P_2O_5$) ............4%

Soluble Potash ($K_2O$) .......8%

    Primary Nutrients from Urea, Ureaform, Ammonium Sulfate, Ammonium Phosphate, and Muriate of Potash.

Potential Acidity 800 lbs. Calcium Carbonate Equivalent per ton. Net Weight 20 lbs.

*Liquid fertilizers are applied by hand-held hose-attached sprayers. Some operators may have trouble applying spray evenly.*

*Spreading fertilizer by hand requires a talented touch. An underhand swing, as above, provides the best results.*

*Drop spreaders are very useful on small lawns. Make sure you overlap applications just enough so that no strips are left unfed.*

## Actual nitrogen

The amount of "actual" nitrogen is a term we have used throughout this book. It is simply a convenient way to say how much fertilizer a lawn should receive, without figuring the specific type or formula of lawn fertilizer you might use. For example, a 100 pound bag of 24-4-8 (24 percent nitrogen) contains 24 pounds of actual nitrogen. A 20 pound bag of 24-4-8 contains 4.8 pounds of actual nitrogen (20 pounds multiplied by .24 equals 4.8 pounds).

If you want to apply 1 pound of actual nitrogen over 1,000 square feet of lawn using this 24-4-8 fertilizer, you would use 4.17 pounds.

The directions on the bag will usually provide instructions as to the proper amount to use. Most labeled instructions follow the basic guideline of recommending application rates that supply approximately one pound of actual nitrogen per 1,000 square feet. There are exceptions; fertilizers with high percentages of W.I.N. or slow release forms of nitrogen are often applied at higher rates.

## Fertilizer and pesticide combinations

In recent years, many combinations of pesticides and fertilizers have become available. Common types contain herbicides for broadleaf weed control or preemergence herbicides for crabgrass control. There are also products that include other pesticides for insect and disease control.

These products do have definite advantages. Considerable time, labor, and equipment are saved if two jobs can be accomplished in one. Less total material is handled and less storage space is required. In addition, the cost of the combined material may be less than the cost of the individual ingredients purchased separately. Most important, the pesticide can often be applied more evenly and closer to the recommended rate than if it was sprayed on the lawn.

The disadvantage of these kinds of products is the difficulty in making applications at the proper time, since the best time to fertilize is not always the best time to control insects or weeds. Be certain the growth cycles of the insects and weeds coincide with combination product applications for best results. A fertilizer combined with a pesticide is most useful if the advantages and limitations are understood.

## When to fertilize

Few gardeners need to be reminded to feed their lawns in spring. It helps a lawn get a head start on pests, weeds, and the summer heat that's soon to come.

By midsummer, heat and light intensity slow down the growth of the cool-season grasses. They usually remain green but are essentially dormant. We recommend, with only a few exceptions, no feeding of the cool-season grasses in mid-summer.

The most important time to fertilize cool-season grasses is in fall. Fall fertilization keeps the grass growing green and longer into cold weather. The lawn is stimulated to become more dense. Fall feeding also gives the lawn a chance to store food that will get it off to a fast start next spring. Not much top growth takes place in fall so a lawn can store food that will get it off to a fast start next spring.

Growth of the warm-season grasses peaks in midsummer then tapers off in fall, continuing at a slower pace until frost. The first sign of spring green comes when the soil is still cold. This is the time when lawn food with quick-acting forms of nitrogen pays off, making grass fully green sooner.

Warm-season grasses can also benefit from fall fertilization, with two exceptions. If winter weeds are a problem, their growth will be further stimulated by the feeding.

A heavy fertilization may also promote a flush of succulent growth that, in some areas, leaves the grass more susceptible to cold injury. Otherwise, fall fertilization will keep the grass green and growing longer in the fall and promote earlier spring green-up.

## Lime

In areas of the country with heavy rainfall, soils are typically acid. Grasses grow poorly in highly acid soils because of nutrient imbalance and toxicity. Acid soil is corrected by adding lime.

*Hand-held broadcast spreaders operate by turning a side-arm crank; the fertilizer flies out from a whirling wheel.*

*Push-type broadcast spreaders are ideal for large lawns. Before using, measure the "throw" to avoid uneven applications.*

The only sure way to know if your lawn needs lime is through a soil test. However, liming is a way of life in many areas. In those areas, you already know your soil needs lime.

Soil acidity is measured by its pH. On a scale of 14, pH 7 is neutral, above 7 is alkaline, and below 7 is acid. If your soil pH is below 5.5, lime is necessary. A soil pH between 5.5 and 7.5 is good for most grasses and 6.8 to 7 is ideal. (Centipedegrass is an important exception: it prefers more acid soil. Add lime if pH is below 4.5 enough to raise pH to 6.)

The easiest and best form of lime for lawns is ground limestone. Your soil test will provide recommended rates. Lime is best applied with a mechanical spreader.

## How to apply fertilizer

The five basic methods of applying fertilizers are shown in the photographs on these pages.

Liquid fertilizers are applied by hand-held or hose-attached sprayers. Their basic faults are difficulty in applying the fertilizer evenly, frequent fills, and the amount of time it takes to apply adequate amounts. Read the directions on both the liquid fertilizer and the sprayer carefully. Rates are set up according to ratios of liquid fertilizer and water added to the sprayer. Also make sure all parts of the sprayer are attached and operational.

You can broadcast dry fertilizer by hand, but it requires a talented touch

to be efficient. It often causes uneven streaking in the lawn. Use this method only in very small areas or if there is no other alternative.

The use of a drop sreader is a very common method to apply a dry fertilizer. It requires more passes than a broadcast spreader, and is most useful on a medium-sized lawn. When using a drop spreader, overlap the wheels enough so no strips are left underfed, but also be careful not to double feed any sections. If this happens, you'll have uneven greening in the lawn, or worse, fertilizer burn.

The use of a broadcast spreader is probably the easiest way of applying a dry fertilizer. There are two types — hand-held and push-wheel models. Each throws the fertilizer pellets over

a wide area via a whirling wheel. Because they require fewer passes to completely cover the lawn, they are easier to use, especially on large lawns. Make sure you measure the throw width so you know how far to space your passes. This can be easily determined by running the spreader over dark-colored pavement for a short distance. (Note: some overlap is necessary for uniform coverage.)

**Spreader settings:** Push-type drop and broadcast spreaders usually have adjustable settings which correspond to application rates on fertilizer bags. Although fairly accurate when the spreaders are new, they should be calibrated (the actual application rate tested) at least once a year. Instructions for doing this are on page 96 of this book. Hand-held broadcast spreaders can be calibrated the same way.

Drop-type fertilizer spreaders are also used to spread seed. Calibration is again necessary to make sure you apply appropriate quantities of seed.

**Application:** The best technique for applying lawn food is to cover the ends of the lawn first, then go back and forth the long way. To avoid double applications, make sure to shut off the spreader as you approach the end strips. Keep the spreader closed while you are turning around, backing up, or stopped. For even and thorough coverage, walk at normal speed and keep the spreader level.

If you do happen to spill or drop extra dry fertilizer in one area, it should be scraped or vacuumed up. The area should then be flooded with water to avoid fertilizer burn.

After fertilizing, brush or wash out the spreader immediately after use to avoid corrosion. Dry thoroughly before storing.

## Nitrogen requirements

| Pounds of nitrogen per year | Warm-season | Cool-season |
|---|---|---|
| 1 to 3 | Carpetgrass Centipedegrass | Hard fescue |
| 2 to 4 | — | Red fescue Chewings fescue Kentucky bluegrass (common) |
| 4 to 6 | Bahiagrass St. Augustinegrass Zoysiagrass | Tall fescue Annual ryegrass Colonial bentgrass Perennial ryegrass |
| 6 to 12 | Bermudagrasses Dichondra | Kentucky bluegrass (improved) Creeping bentgrass |

These rates show the range for grasses with a long growing season. Lower rates would apply to northern and eastern areas with short seasons.

# Lawn renovation

If your lawn deteriorates to the point that routine cultural practices such as mowing, fertilization, watering, and weed control, do not give the desired response, it is probably time to renovate. By renovating, it is possible to renew your lawn without going to the trouble of completely rebuilding the lawn.

The Cooperative Extension Service of Kansas State University says: "Many established lawns become thin, weedy, or have been damaged by insects or disease, but the homeowner does not want to plow it up and start over from bare soil. Cool-season lawns can be improved without destroying the existing grass through a process called over-seeding or re-seeding. There are some key operations to perform in order for over-seeding to be successful. Merely scattering seed over the lawn rarely results in seedling establishment and survival."

Renovation, or re-seeding, as Kansas State University calls it, may involve the use of heavy equipment available from a rental yard (see page 57). There are also many lawn service companies that specialize in this kind of service. In any case, renovation is a chance to repair mistakes made when you first planted your lawn, or amend problems that have gotten out of hand.

## Thatch

If you need to renovate your lawn because of thatch build-up, you have a lot of company. The spongy feel to lawns with heavy thatch is a result of a thick layer of slowly decomposing stems, roots, and debris. A thin layer of thatch, ¼ to ½ inch, may actually be beneficial because it buffers soil temperature and adds to the lawn's resilience. This reduces the compaction of soil that results from heavy use. If thick enough, thatch can actually be water repellent or "hydrophopic." A conscientious waterer may think he or she is watering enough, but actually the water never reaches the soil. Grass roots that grow in the thatch layer instead of the soil are naturally less drought resistant, since the moisture in the thatch evaporates much faster. Insects and disease find thatch a particularly suitable place to inhabit. Since water cannot penetrate, neither can pest control materials. Finally, variable thicknesses and density of thatch make scalping by mowers almost inevitable.

**Why thatch accumulates:** Thatch accumulates fastest in lawns composed of spreading-type grasses. Notorious thatch builders include warm-season grasses such as bermuda and zoysiagrass.

Pennsylvania State University says this about cool-season grass thatch build-up: "The rate of thatch build-up is dependent on several factors. All turfgrasses will thatch if given the opportunity. Bentgrass, because of its vigorous growth and habit of growth, builds up thatch quite rapidly. 'Merion' Kentucky bluegrass is probably the most notorious thatch developer of the general lawn grasses because of its rapid growth and resistance to decomposition of the clippings. Red fescue is a slow grower, but its leaves and stems are extremely resistant to decomposition. Red fescue requires a longer period of time to accumulate thatch than does 'Merion' Kentucky bluegrass."

**What to do about thatch.** Soil penetrants, or wetting agents, only offer short term reduction of thatch symptoms. They counteract its hydrophopic character, but the effect is shortlived and definitely not a cure. Bacterial agents that supposedly break down thatch have also proven to be of little value.

There are attachments for rotary mowers that may be helpful in thatch removal. A thatch hand rake that has knifelike blades instead of the usual, hard steel teeth can be used. As a last resort, a sod cutter can remove especially thick thatch if it has built up to impossible levels. (Note: this is only applicable for grasses that have underground runners). Adjust the sod cutter to cut just above the soil level instead of below. Fixed, flail, and spring tooth mowers are also available for dethatching.

The most accepted way to dethatch a home lawn is by vertical mowing. The vertical mower is a specialized machine that thins the grass and brings much of the thatch to the surface of the lawn. You then sweep, rake, or vacuum this material from the lawn.

In order for dethatching to be effective, the depth of penetration of the blade should be adjusted so the blade will completely penetrate through the thatch layer and into the soil under the thatch.

These recommendations are valuable for realizing the recuperative powers of different grasses, but adjusting blades on a vertical mower is usually difficult. If you rent one it is

*The easiest way to repair a damaged section of lawn is to patch it with a piece of sod custom cut to fit the area.*

probably impossible. Make only one pass on a slow-to-recover grass if you cannot properly adjust the blades.

**Dethatch timing:** The best time to dethatch is just before the lawn's most vigorous growth of the season. For warm-season grasses, dethatching should be done with the beginning of warm weather in late spring. Cool-season grasses grow best in spring and fall. The prime time to dethatch is in the fall; the second best time is early spring.

## About aeration

Roots need air as well as water and nutrients for growth. Lawns, especially those that receive heavy use, can develop compacted, air-deficient soil. Compacted soil also restricts water absorption. A foot-path worn into a lawn is compaction. To correct the many problems of compacted soil, lawn professionals have developed specialized tools and techniques.

Correcting compacted soil is described by a variety of names, including "hole punching," "coring," and "aerification." All are based on the same principle: Hollow metal tubes ¼ to ¾ inch in diameter are pushed into the soil by foot or machine, to a depth of 3 to 4 inches, sometimes deeper. The soil should be *moist* when doing this, not too wet, not too dry. Take a look at the photographs (next page) of the aerifier used on one of our lawns.

## Overseeding in winter

The only disadvantage of the warm-season grasses is their winter dormancy. Scientists say that it is caused by a combination of low temperatures and winter sunlight. Whatever the cause, most lawn owners prefer all-year green color. Lawns can either be painted green or overseeded (see "lawn tips," page 92 to 93).

**Grasses for overseeding:** Annual ryegrass is suitable for overseeding dormant bermudagrass. The seed is inexpensive and widely available. Use it heavily: about 10 pounds per 1,000 square feet.

Turf-type perennial ryegrass is excellent for overseeding. The color is a dark green and the growth rate is slower than that of annual ryegrass, resulting in less mowing.

The fine fescues are also good for overseeding. Use them alone or in combination with the ryegrasses.

To be successful in overseeding, close mowing, dethatching, and (if possible) aerification are recommended. These steps help ensure close contact of seed and soil. As an alternative, mow close to the soil with a heavy, reel-type mower. Seed, and finish with a top dressing of peat moss or similar organic material. Don't forget to water frequently until the new grass is firmly rooted into the soil.

The following spring, encourage the growth of the permanent lawn grass at the expense of the winter cover. Just before the late spring flush of growth, vertical mow again or mow close and fertilize. This will be enough of a shock to the winter cover and enough of a boost to the main lawngrass to reestablish.

## Patching

Patching involves removing the weedy, dead, or damaged section of the lawn and replacing it with a piece of sod or by reseeding. It is always done with the same variety of grass as the present lawn. Many nurseries normally stock a small amount of sod just for this purpose.

Dig out the damaged area and loosen the soil underneath. If spilled gasoline or herbicide is the cause of the dead spot, remove several inches of the soil and replace it. Bring the underlying soil to proper grade and cut a piece of sod to fit.

Of course, patching can be done with seed, too. The process is the same as with any new seeding. Regardless of the method, remember to give close attention to watering for several weeks.

## A renovating experience

On the following two pages we show the steps we took to renovate one of our lawns. We chose seed rather than sod to get the full growing experience.

The lawn had many weeds, including unwanted bermudagrass and oxalis, requiring the most drastic kind of renovation. The entire lawn area was sprayed with a systemic herbicide, glyphosate. One week later we dethatched, aerified, and seeded.

We did not take a soil test, since it had been tested many times previously. However, it is wise to know exactly what type of soil you have. See pages 80 to 89 for a list of soil testing agencies.

---

*A trip to a rental yard near Santa Rosa, California, produced the photograph of lawn equipment for rent. Moving clockwise from the upper left corner is a sickle or bar mower (a). They are perfect for that empty lot overgrown with weeds. A high-wheel rotary mower (b) cuts higher than most rotaries — about 4 inches — and is much easier to maneuver over rough terrain. A sod cutter (c) can be useful two ways. One, you can strip off old turf, or two, remove thatch. Riding mowers (d) are perfect for big, relatively smooth lawns. The type pictured has a rotary mower mounted midsection. Lawn aerators, (e) are used to remove cores of soil. This provides air in the grass root zone. As soil becomes compacted, the amount of air space in the soil is reduced. A vertical mower (f) goes by at least two other names: dethatcher or lawn comb. This piece of equipment cuts perpendicular to the surface of the lawn, slicing deep into thatch. After one pass it's easy to rake up the thatch debris. Two types of edgers, power and manual, are pictured (g). Hand edgers are fine for most trimming needs. Power types are an advantage for large lawns. The two lawn rollers (h) may look similar but have completely different uses. The barrel type is filled with water to reduce the fluffiness of freshly rototilled soil. and to provide good contact between seed or sod and the soil. (Use it half or less than half full.) The other roller is used to spread bulky organic topdressing materials such as peat moss, manure, or composted bark. It is shown in action on page 27. Besides vertical mowers and riding mowers, most rental yards will have a variety of common lawn mower types (i). You can rent a heavy reel mower for the one or two times you need to cut the lawn extra low for thatch removal.*

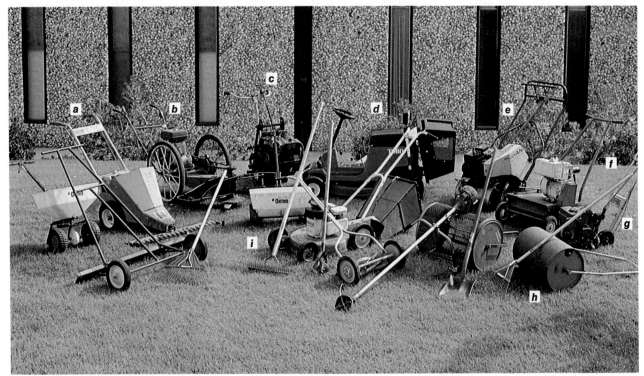

# Lawn renovation

### Remove undesirable weeds and grasses 1

The lawn at the right contained bermudagrass as well as various broadleaf weeds. The entire lawn was killed using glyphosate. Herbicides, such as 2-4, D, are chemicals that would be used if the lawn was infested with broadleaf weeds. Always read labels carefully when using herbicides. Be sure materials are safe to use around trees and shrubs. Never use pre-emergent weed controls, unless specifically recommended, prior to reseeding. Make sure the chemical leaves no residue that may harm young grasses.

### Using a vertical mower, verticut the existing lawn 2

In order to have contact between seed and soil, it is necessary to remove as much thatch as possible. Vertical mowers remove thatch like mechanical rakes, slicing vertically into the soil with knives or tines. Notice the grooves that the vertical mower leaves in the soil. Use the vertical mower on a damp lawn, never dry or soaking wet. For the best results, go over the lawn twice in opposite directions.

Low mowing and vigorous raking with a steel rake may be sufficient to remove thatch from small lawns. However, it is a tedious process and much less efficient than a vertical mower. Dethatching attachments are also available for rotary mowers, but these are not as thorough.

### Rake up debris 3

Thoroughly rake up any loose debris left by vertical mowing. (There can be quite a lot.) This guarantees the all-important contact between seed and soil. The debris should be discarded if chemicals were used previously. Otherwise, the dead grass and thatch removed by vertical mowing make an excellent addition to the compost pile or as a mulch for the vegetable garden.

## 4 Aerate the soil

Aerators remove small cores of soil from the lawn which allows air, water, and nutrients to pass freely to the roots. Aeration is best done on a damp lawn. Remove the soil cores by raking, or shred with a rotary mower, and use them to level any uneven spots.

This lawn had several low spots that made mowing difficult. If there are high and low spots in the new seedbed, add a good topsoil or peatmoss and sand, and level with a rake. It may be necessary to flatten high spots with a steel rake. If crushed soil cores left over from aeration are used for leveling, it may be desirable to blend them with additional organic matter.

## 5 Add lime, fertilize, and sow seed

If liming is a way of life in your area, this is the time to do it. It's also the time to apply a complete balanced fertilizer.

If a good percentage of desirable grasses are present, it may not be necessary to reseed, just fertilize and water heavily. If you do seed or use vegetative methods to re-establish, follow a good watering program.

Right after planting is a critical time in the re-establishment of healthy turf. It may be necessary to water several times a day in hot weather in order to keep the seed, sprigs, or stolons moist until they become established.

## 6 The end result, a renovated lawn

This photograph was taken just six weeks after the renovation process was completed. It's important to stress, however, that lawn care doesn't end here. In order to keep problems from re-occurring and to keep the lawn looking its best, you need to follow an efficient program of fertilizing, watering, mowing, and dethatching.

# Lawn weeds

Weeds are simply plants in the wrong place. The finest lawngrass plant is a weed in the vegetable garden and, likewise, dandelions are cultivated in some of the best vegetable gardens.

Most lawn weeds are easily eliminated. Mowing at the right height, fertilizing adequately, and good watering practices will go a long way in achieving a weed-free lawn.

A healthy lawn will not be troubled much by weeds. Since problems and questions do come up, we've put together the following short course on weeds. The following five pages contain photographs of the most common lawn weeds, and their controls.

## First, some definitions

*Annual:* A plant that lives only one year.

*Perennial:* A plant that lives for two or more years.

*Herbicide:* A chemical used to kill plants.

*Pre-emergence:* A term used to describe herbicides that are effective against germinating seeds — before the plant emerges through the soil surface.

*Post-emergence:* A term used to describe herbicides that are effective after a plant breaks through the soil surface.

*Contact herbicide:* Kills plant parts covered by the spray. Affects only above-ground parts.

*Systemic herbicide:* Absorbed by the plant to circulate inside it, killing all parts, including the roots.

## How weeds get in the lawn

Weed seeds are in most soils by the millions. They wait, dormant, until brought to the soil surface or until the lawngrass dies, when light and moisture start them growing. Some seeds can remain alive in the soil for many years. That is why some weed treatments are useful before you plant.

## How to control lawn weeds

The more weeds you eliminate before planting will naturally leave fewer to battle later on. Following is one of the best methods of weed elimination. Simply keep the soil bare and moist for three or four months, and either till, or spray with a contact herbicide every three weeks, as the weed seeds germinate. If it's awkward to leave your soil bare that long, try another method.

Fumigation is another pre-plant weed treatment. It too, usually involves time — at least three weeks. (Check the label directions.) Vapam makes a gas that kills many weed seeds and other soil organisms. It works very well, but is neither inexpensive or simple to apply. Also, it may harm nearby tree or shrub roots if roots extend into the treated area. Methyl bromide is another soil fumigant which works well and is fast (two to three days), but it is the most dangerous one to use, so much so, we don't recommend it for home lawns, unless used by a professional. A special permit is usually required. The only other pre-plant weed control method is the use of a pre-emergence herbicide. Some types will discriminate between the weed and the lawn grass seed; one is Tupersan.

## Weed killers

Weeds are of two types: broadleaf and narrowleaf. Broadleaf weeds have more obvious, showy flowers. Their leaves have a network of small veins originating from a principal point or vein which often divides the leaf in half. Dandelion and knotweed are typical broadleaf weeds. Grassy weeds are narrowleaf types. They usually have hollow stems and long, narrow leaf blades with parallel veins. Foxtail and crabgrass are common narrowleaf weeds.

Another weed type, much less common, are the sedges. They look similar to grasses, but have triangular stems. It is important to stress the differences between these weed types. An herbicide that kills one type may not even affect the other. Also, it is particularly important to pay strict attention to labeled instructions. Many weed killers or pest controls are only effective within certain temperature ranges and stages of plant maturity. Be very careful when applying any chemical products. Don't spray on windy days, and keep children away when you do spray.

Weed killers are either pre-emergent or post-emergent. The post-emergent types are further categorized as either contact or systemic. Chemical names are listed first. Trade names follow in parenthesis.

## Pre-emergents

**Benefin** (Balan). Controls annual grasses in most lawns. Don't use on bentgrass. It will prevent all seeds from germinating for up to eight weeks.

**Bensulide** (Betasan). Another control for annual grasses and certain broad-

leaves. Don't try to reseed for four months after application.

**DCPA** (Dacthal). Especially effective on germinating grasses and seed of certain broadleaf species, including chickweed and purslane. Don't use on new lawns and don't reseed for 10 to 12 weeks after using.

**Siduron** (Tupersan). Effectively controls weedy grasses such as crab grass, foxtail, and barnyard grass. It has the unique quality of not interfering with the germination of cool-season grasses such as Kentucky bluegrass.

## Post-emergents

**Cacodylic acid** (Contax, Phytar-560). Kills only upon contact. Very effective although repeat treatments are necessary before it will kill tough perennials such as bermudagrass. Kills all green-growing leaf tissue, does not move within plants to roots. Often used to clear lawns of existing growth, prior to renovation.

**2,4-D.** Widely available in many forms and products. It is essentially a growth-influencing hormone that singles out the broadleaf weeds in the lawn, killing them, without damaging most lawn grasses.

**MCPP** (Mecoprop). Related and very similar to 2,4-D but safer to use on new lawns or sensitive grasses such as bentgrass or St. Augustinegrass.

**Dicamba** (Banvel). Particularly effective against clover, beggarweed, chickweed, knotweed, and red sorrel. It is a hormone-type weed killer as 2,4-D but is taken up through roots as well as through leaves. Be very careful using it around trees and shrubs or in areas where roots underlay the area to be treated.

**Dalapon** (Dowpon). Effective against all grasses. Usually used for spot treatment of undesired clumps of bermudagrass or tall fescue. Use in the West to eliminate bermudagrass from dichondra lawns. Use carefully, excessive rates can damage dichondra.

**DSMA, MSMA, MAMA** (available in many combinations under several trade names). Used to control grassy weeds such as crabgrass and foxtail. They kill mostly by foliage activity. Effective against hard-to-kill nutsedges.

**Glyphosate** (Roundup). Non-selective and systemic: It will kill both grasses and broadleaf weeds. It is the best herbicide for control of bermudagrass, and is also useful against other perennial grassy weeds.

**Annual bluegrass** or **Poa annua.** Narrowleaf. Annual.

**Season of fast growth:** Prefers cool weather of spring and fall. Tends to die out in summer.

**Pre-emergence control:** DCPA, bensulide, and benefin. Apply in early August. Several applications may be necessary.

**Post-emergence control:** None.

**Bermudagrass, devilgrass.** Narrowleaf. Perennial.

**Season of fast growth:** Summer. Grows fast when temperatures are high.

**Pre-emergence control:** None.

**Post-emergence control:** Dalapon is one of the best. The newer glyphosate will also control bermudagrass but may be hard to find in most areas.

**Comments:** Where bermudagrass is well adapted to the climate, *it is your lawn* or a troublesome weed.

**Crabgrass.** Narrowleaf. Annual.

**Season of fast growth:** A summer weed. Begins in early spring and grows fast until seed heads form in late summer to fall.

**Pre-emergence control:** Products containing DCPA, benefin, bensulide, and siduron. Weed killer must be applied in spring before seedlings appear. Check ''Lawns in your area,'' pages 80 to 89, and ''Lawn calendar,'' pages 92 to 93.

**Post-emergence control:** DSMA, MSMA, MAMA. Apply when weeds are small and much easier to control. One or more repeat treatments at 7- to 10-day intervals may be necessary.

**Dallisgrass.** Narrowleaf. Perennial.

**Season of fast growth:** Dallisgrass is a summer weed, but will grow all year in mild climates.

**Pre-emergence control:** None.

**Post-emergence control:** Use DSMA, MAMA, or MSMA every ten days or as the label directs as a spot spray. Check label before using on St. Augustine, centipede or bahiagrass.

**Comments:** Thrives in low wet areas. Try to drain the soil first for control. Bahiagrass is a close relative and sometimes infests bermudagrass lawns. Similar treatment will control.

**Dandelion.** Broadleaf. Perennial.

*Season of fast growth:* Spring and fall.

*Pre-emergence control:* None.

*Post-emergence control:* Sprays containing 2,4-D or mecoprop are very effective. Apply during spring or fall when growth is active, but before yellow flowers appear. Spray or treat on a windless day when temperatures are above 60°F. but less than 80°F.

*Comments:* Improved turf varieties usually resist dandelion invasion quite well.

**Dock.** Broadleaf. Perennial.

*Season of fast growth:* Spring and fall.

*Pre-emergence control:* None.

*Post-emergence control:* Use 2, 4-D, mecoprop, or dicamba mid-spring or mid-fall.

**English daisy.** Broadleaf. Perennial.

*Season of fast growth:* Cool weather of spring and fall. All season if protected from drought and high heat.

*Pre-emergence control:* None.

*Post-emergence control:* A difficult to control weed; 2,4-D and mecoprop will give fair control. Apply in late spring.

**Henbit.** Broadleaf. Annual.

*Season of fast growth:* Spring and fall.

*Pre-emergence control:* None.

*Post-emergence control:* Use 2,4-D or mecoprop in fall or spring. Two applications may be required.

*Comments:* This weed is from the mint family, you'll notice its four-sided stem. It shows up in late winter or early spring.

**Knotweed.** Broadleaf. Annual.

***Season of fast growth:*** Early spring through early fall.

***Pre-emergence control:*** None.

***Post-emergence control:*** Mecoprop or dicamba are the favored treatment anytime throughout season of most active growth beginning in early spring.

***Comments:*** A common weed in hard, compacted soils. Thorough aerification may help.

**Mallow, cheeseweed.** Broadleaf. Annual.

***Season of fast growth:*** Has a long growing season. Gets started in early spring and survives through fall. A difficult weed to control.

***Pre-emergence control:*** None.

***Post-emergence control:*** Use 2,4-D, mecoprop, or dicamba mid- to late-spring.

**Mouse-ear chickweed.** Broadleaf. Perennial.

***Season of fast growth:*** Cool weather of spring or fall.

***Pre-emergence control:*** None.

***Post-emergence control:*** Mecoprop. Apply in fall or in early spring when temperatures are between 60° and 70° F.

**Oxalis.** Broadleaf. Perennial.

***Season of fast growth:*** Spring and late summer to fall.

***Pre-emergence control:*** None.

***Post-emergence control:*** Products containing 2,4-D and dicamba may be used. Apply in spring or fall on a day when the wind is still and air temperatures will remain above 60°F, but below 80°F. In many areas, late summer to fall treatment is most effective. Not easy to kill; usually requires several treatments.

**Plantain.** Broadleaf. Perennial.

***Season of fast growth:*** A cool-season weed. Forms rosettes with prominently veined leaves.

***Pre-emergence control:*** None.

***Post-emergence control:*** 2,4-D or mecoprop are very effective, applied spring or fall before formation of flower spikes.

**Purslane.** Broadleaf. Annual.

***Season of fast growth:*** Summer.

***Pre-emergence control:*** DCPA applied early to mid-spring.

***Post-emergence control:*** Use 2,4-D mid- to late-summer.

**Quackgrass.** Narrowleaf. Perennial.

***Season of fast growth:*** Spring and fall.

***Pre-emergence treatment:*** None.

***Post-emergence control:*** No selective control. Spot treat with dalapon or glyphosate.

***Comments:*** Underground stems are vigorous, even digging out by hand is rarely successful.

**Spotted spurge.** Broadleaf. Annual.

***Season of fast growth:*** Most aggressive growth is from late spring through early fall. A summer weed.

***Pre-emergence control:*** Use DCPA or siduron in early spring before germination then again in mid-summer.

***Post-emergence control:*** Products containing 2,4-D and dicamba may be used.

***Comments:*** Minor damage may result to turfgrasses from summer treatments.

**Tall fescue.** Narrowleaf. Perennial.

***Season of fast growth:*** A perennial, but grows fastest in spring and fall.

***Pre-emergence control:*** None.

***Post-emergence control:*** Spot treat only. Use either repeated sprays with a contact herbicide or dalapon. Glyphosate applied any time the weed is actively growing will also give good control.

***Comments:*** Frequently confused with crabgrass. Can be dug out by hand.

**Veronica, speedwell.** Broadleaf. Annual.

***Season of fast growth:*** Spring and fall.

***Pre-emergence control:*** None.

***Post-emergence control:*** 2,4-D is effective. Spray in fall. Two applications may be necessary.

***Comments:*** Dense patches of veronica become established below mowing height. A tough weed to kill. Several slightly varying species. Flowers are light blue and seed pods are heart-shaped.

**White clover.** Broadleaf. Perennial.

***Season of fast growth:*** Cool seasons of fall and spring. Profuse flowering in early summer.

***Pre-emergence control:*** None.

***Post-emergence control:*** Mecoprop or dicamba in spring or fall. Choose a warm and windless day.

**Wild onion, wild garlic.** Broadleaf. Perennial.

***Season of fast growth:*** Spring to mid-summer.

***Pre-emergence control:*** None.

***Post-emergence control:*** 2,4-D or dicamba. May need several treatments. Herbicide-impregnated bars are more effective. Best used in late fall when weeds are still small; once mature, difficult to control.

***Comments:*** Wild onion differs from wild garlic in two ways: Wild onions do not produce the underground bulbs common to wild garlic. And, garlic has a hollow leaf; the onion leaf is not hollow.

# Insects and pests

There's a patch of dead grass next to the driveway or a dead spot under the oak — was it caused by insects? The most difficult and important part of any lawn problem is diagnosing the cause.

Hundreds of kinds of insects and similar creatures live in a typical lawn. Some are so tiny they're hardly visible; or others are quite large. Most do little damage to the lawn itself, and you're not even aware of their presence. Other insects which are troublesome to people make their homes in lawns, but do not damage the grass. Fleas and ticks are in this category. But only a few serious lawn pests, such as sod webworm, the grubs of various beetles, and chinch bugs can destroy a lawn within a short time if conditions are right for their development.

The questions are: How to tell if the problem is caused by insects or a disease (or something else, such as gasoline or a dog). And if it is caused by insects, how can the damage be stopped.

## Diagnosing the problem

In trying to discover the source of lawn damage, the easiest and most reliable method is to look, and look closely. Get down on your hands and knees and chances are, you will be able to see the pest in action. Some appear only at night, or only in a shady spot, or in a sunny corner. Specific habits and characteristics of the most common lawn pests are noted on the following pages.

Discovering insects in your lawn does not necessarily mean you have to spray. If there is a problem try to link in some definite way the symptom to the pest. For example, look for the green pellet-like droppings left by sod webworm. Remember too that damage is hardly visible until the pest population has built up to a considerable extent.

Many insects are only troublesome to certain kinds of grass. For instance, chinch bugs are by far most damaging to St. Augustinegrass. Wireworms rarely attack any grasses besides bahia or centipede. There are many examples like these. So to the extent possible, choose a grass that's not bothered or at least doesn't have a number one enemy.

Grow a healthy lawn. We don't intend to make that sound simple or the solution to all problems, but a well-maintained lawn will be much less subject to serious insect damage.

It is also able to recover quickly if problems do occur.

Finally, if your lawn is a perfect, frequently watered and fertilized putter's delight, be prepared for some extra pest-related chores. In such a prime environment, more insect eggs are laid and more will survive.

## Controlling lawn pests with chemicals

Insecticides are not the only answer to lawn pest problems. But, if and when you decide they are necessary, we feel you should know about them. There are many forms of insecticides available. If used properly, they are relatively harmless.

Here are some brief descriptions of insecticides commonly used by homeowners to control lawn pests. For the sake of simplification, we have listed the most frequently used trade or chemical name.

**Aspon:** This is a good control for chinch bugs and sod webworm. It works fast and is effective up to two months. Water the lawn before spraying, then withhold water for two or three days to permit the chemical to do its job. Keep off the lawn until the chemical has been washed into the soil.

**Baygon:** Similar to Sevin (see below). Frequently used in baits. Controls chinch bugs, earwigs, leafhoppers.

**Carbaryl:** Also known as Sevin. This chemical has been around a long time and is available in a wide variety of forms from many manufacturers. It has several uses for home lawn insect control.

**Diazinon:** Like carbaryl, widely available in many forms. One of the best for grub control. Protects against

several lawn pests up to four to six weeks.

**Chlorpyrifos:** This is more commonly known by its trade name, Dursban. It provides effective control on chinch bugs, grubs, and sod webworm and many other insect pests as well. It remains effective for four to six weeks.

**Metaldehyde:** Look for this ingredient in slug and snail baits. Use it where snails hide, such as around ground covers. Both snails and slugs hide in cool, moist areas during the day and come out at night. They love new lawns and dichondra.

**Methoxyclor:** A common ingredient in many spray mixes. Generally, it is very useful and has about a two-month residual.

**Mesurol:** This is a very effective killer of slugs and snails. Lightly water the area before spreading the bait.

**Milky disease:** (Biological control) This is a disease natural to Japanese beetle grubs. It has no effect on other kinds of grubs or any other insects. It is established in soils over a period of years where Japanese beetles are present. It is slow to establish and control is not one hundred percent, but it will keep the beetles in check.

***Bacillus thuringensis:*** (Biological control) Similar to milky spore disease in that it is very specific. It will kill only caterpillars (butterfly and moth larvae). Very useful in many situations, although it is not widely used on lawns.

Of course, the best information on these and other pest control products is on the product label. We must stress, read the label in the nursery or garden shop before purchase and again, carefully, before use.

---

## Identifying pest damage

Lawn damaging insects can be conveniently grouped according to where they are most active, above or below the ground, and the type of damage they do. Control methods are different for each group.

**Live above the soil surface and suck plant juices — chinch bugs, leafhoppers, spider mites, and similar pests.**

**To control:**
✓ Mow the lawn.
✓ Remove clippings.
✓ Water heavily.
✓ Wait until grass blades are dry, then apply insecticide according to label directions. Do not water for two days.

**Live at the soil surface and feed on leaves — sod webworms, cutworms, armyworms, and fiery skipper larvae.**

**To control:**
✓ Mow the lawn.
✓ Remove clippings.
✓ Water heavily.
✓ Wait until grass blades are dry, then apply insecticide according to label directions. Best applied in late afternoon when insects are active.
✓ Do not water for two days.
✓ Fertilize to aid in recovery of the lawn, if the season is appropriate.

**Live below the soil surface and feed on roots — grubs, wireworms, ground pearls.**

**To control:**
✓ Mow the lawn.
✓ Remove clippings.
✓ Apply recommended insecticide according to label directions. Water heavily immediately after spraying, but not so much that the insecticide washes away.
✓ Fertilize to aid in recovery of the lawn if the season is appropriate.

# Sod webworm

**Symptom:** In late spring look for small dead patches 1 to 2 inches in diameter among the normal growing grass. By midsummer. these may be large dead patches. The most severe damage usually occurs in July and August. Sod webworms chew grass blades off just above the thatch line and pull the blades into a silken tunnel to eat them. Eventually, the small patches will coalesce, forming large, irregular dead patches.

**Description:** The adult form of the webworm is a buff colored moth with a wing span of about one inch. They fly in a jerky, zig-zag pattern, just a few feet above the lawn. The moths don't damage the lawn but they drop eggs into the grass that, upon hatching develop into very hungry caterpillars.

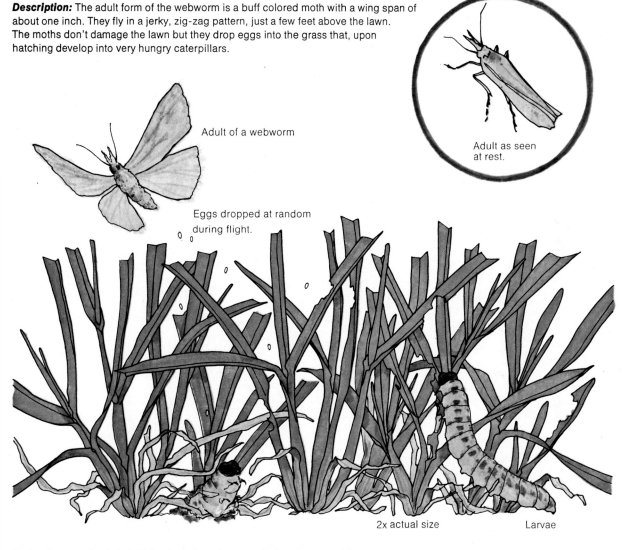

Adult of a webworm

Adult as seen at rest.

Eggs dropped at random during flight.

2x actual size

Larvae

Sod webworms feed at night. Look for them by carefully breaking apart the damaged areas with your fingers. Other evidence is their green-tan excrement, little pellets about the size of a pin head. Also, flocks of birds feeding on the lawn may indicate large populations of sod webworm. When sod webworms are suspected, they can be forced to the surface of the grass by drenching 1 square foot area with 1 gallon of soapy water.
(Use ¼ cup of laundry or household detergent per gallon.)

**Control:** Aspon, diazinon, Dursban, Sevin, Baygon.

**Pupa** **Eggs**

**Young grubs** feeding in soil. Apply insecticide at this stage, usually late July.

**Maturing grubs** move deeper into soil during winter.

**Adult grubs** return to surface in spring to feed and pupate.

1 ½ x actual size

## Japanese beetle life cycle

Checking for grubs.

## Grubs

**Symptoms:** Distinct brown patches, usually irregular in shape. Since the grubs eat grass roots, the dead grass pulls loose easily. If the dead patch of grass rolls back easily like a section of carpet, you can be pretty sure it is caused by below-ground grubs. They are most damaging in late spring or early fall. If you see more than two C-shaped grubs in a square foot area, the lawn should be treated. As with sod webworm, another sign of grubs is unusual numbers of birds or moles around the lawn. They know the grubs are there and are looking to make a dinner of them.

June beetle    May beetle    Masked chafer    *Ataenus spretulus*    European chafer (top) *Phyllophaga crinita*

Actual size

**Description:** Grubs are the larvae of many kinds of beetles. They are whitish or grayish in color with brown heads and dark hind parts. The adult beetles appear in late spring or summer and feed on shade trees or garden shrubs.

**Control:** If your lawn is already infested with grubs, keep in mind they are insulated by a layer of grass leaves and soil. The insecticide must get to this depth in the soil by repeated heavy waterings. Use products that contain diazinon or Dursban.

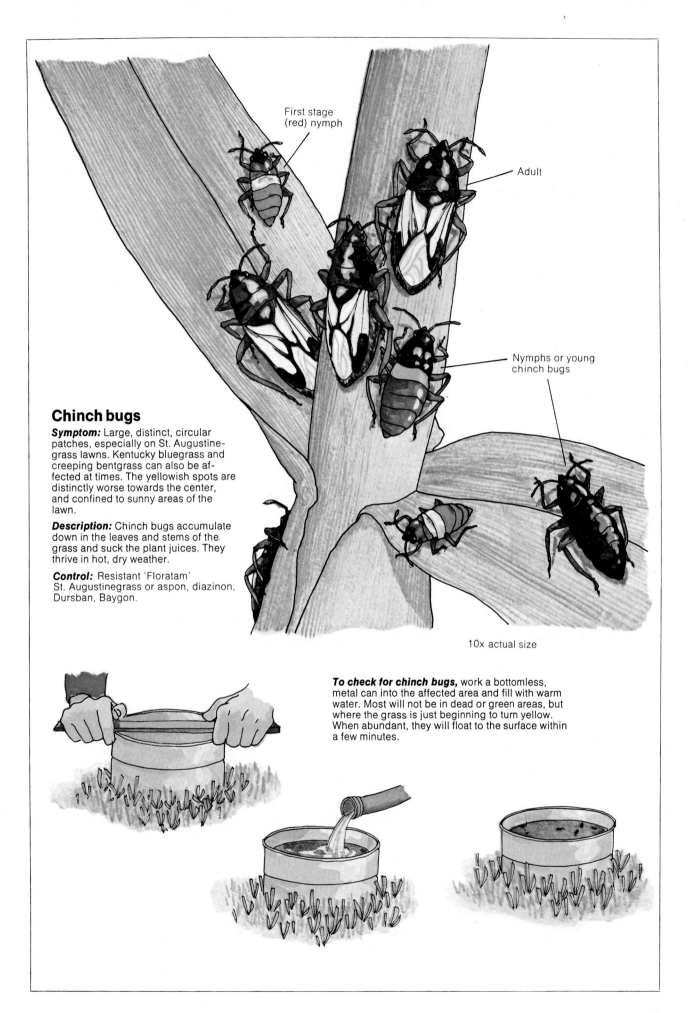

First stage (red) nymph

Adult

Nymphs or young chinch bugs

## Chinch bugs

**Symptom:** Large, distinct, circular patches, especially on St. Augustine-grass lawns. Kentucky bluegrass and creeping bentgrass can also be affected at times. The yellowish spots are distinctly worse towards the center, and confined to sunny areas of the lawn.

**Description:** Chinch bugs accumulate down in the leaves and stems of the grass and suck the plant juices. They thrive in hot, dry weather.

**Control:** Resistant 'Floratam' St. Augustinegrass or aspon, diazinon, Dursban, Baygon.

10x actual size

**To check for chinch bugs,** work a bottomless, metal can into the affected area and fill with warm water. Most will not be in dead or green areas, but where the grass is just beginning to turn yellow. When abundant, they will float to the surface within a few minutes.

## Billbug

**Symptom:** A small and distinct circular pattern becomes yellowish or brown. Adult billbugs feed on stems, while grubs of billbugs feed on roots. Most damage is caused in late summer. Grass stems within the dead areas lift easily out of the soil.

**Description:** Different species of billbugs prefer different types of grass. In the southern-most regions, bermuda and zoysiagrass are commonly attacked, while in the northern regions, Kentucky bluegrass is preferred.

**Control.** Use an insecticide such as diazinon or Baygon in mid-summer if you find more than one billbug grub per square foot.

2½ x actual size

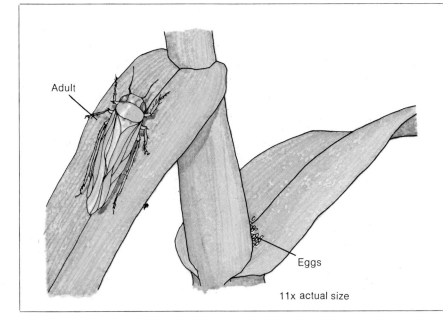

## Leafhopper

**Symptom:** These tiny insects are nearly always present to some degree on the surface of lawns. When severe, they can wipe out a newly seeded lawn and cause a mature lawn to look bleached and unhealthy.

**Description:** They are tiny, even when full grown. Their color is usually green, but may be yellow or grey. If your lawn has a lot of them, each step through the grass will kick a swarm.

**Control:** Insecticide treatments are usually not necessary, they may be more of a nuisance to you than the lawn. Diazinon will effectively control them if necessary.

11x actual size

## Clover mite

**Symptom:** You may first become aware of these pests when they move inside your house looking for a warm place to spend winter. They live primarily on clover and similar plants in the lawn.

**Description:** Tiny green to red-brown spiders that live and feed on the under-surface of grass blades. Sometimes their webbing is visible.

**Control:** Usually kept in check by other insects, predators or insecticide treatments for other pests. If treatment is necessary, use diazinon or Kelthane, a miticide, as the label directs.

50x actual size

## Armyworms, cutworms, and fiery skipper

**Symptoms:** These three moth larvae chew off the grass blades above the soil surface. The damage they cause is very similar to sod webworm. Armyworms cause round, bare areas in lawns. If there are many of them, the grass will be eaten to the soil level. Cutworms also feed on the grass leaves, cutting them off near the surface. Fiery skippers are usually a minor problem, but can be serious pests of bentgrass and bermudagrass lawns, especially hybrid bermuda. They can also be a problem on bluegrass lawns in some areas.

**Descriptions:** Skippers are easy to distinguish from other pests. They're about an inch long and brownish yellow, with very distinct dark brown heads and thin necks. Cutworms are plump, smooth, and almost always curled when you find them. They're usually brown to nearly black, but some are spotted and some are striped. Armyworms are yellowish white and have an upsidedown "Y" on their head.

**Control:** Products that contain diazinon, Dursban, or Sevin are all useful.

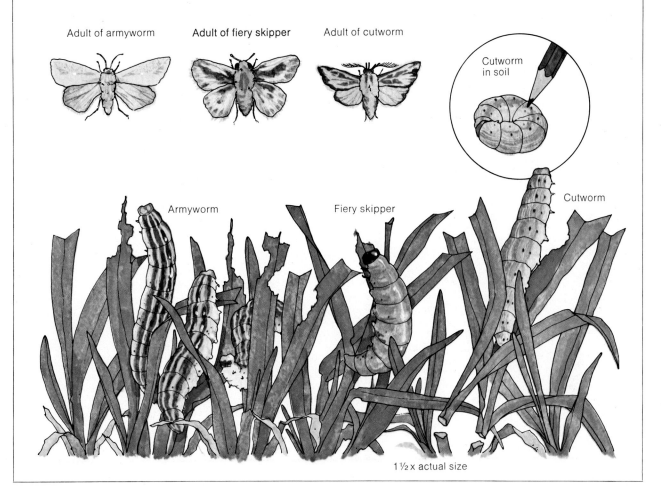

Adult of armyworm    Adult of fiery skipper    Adult of cutworm

Cutworm in soil

Armyworm    Fiery skipper    Cutworm

1½ x actual size

## Nuisance pests

### Brown dog tick
This pest is most common to lawns that are near wooded areas. Ticks will be most active in spring and early summer. *DON'T* try to get them off with a hot match. Diazinon, Dursban or Sevin are good lawn sprays.

1½ x

### Ants
Ants are a problem in lawns because of the nest mounds they make, not because they feed directly on, or otherwise harm the grass. Diazinon granules, Dursban, or diazinon sprays will control them for up to two months.

2½ x

### Gnats
A type of tiny fly, they're similar to mosquitos in many ways; most need water to lay eggs. They can be annoying when they swarm around the lawn. The best treatment is a fogging spray.

5x

1½ x

50x

4x

### Earwigs
These hard, dark reddish brown insects hide in dark places during the day. Their pincers aren't nearly as dangerous as they look; they're only useful against other earwigs. Baits containing Baygon, scattered in the evening, are very effective, or spray with diazinon, Dursban, or Sevin.

### Chiggers
Chiggers are not insects. They are actually tiny spiders or mites. Their eggs are laid in the soil. After hatching, the larvae crawl up onto the grass or weeds waiting for an animal to brush by. Repellents containing diethyltoluamide are effective as well as sprays of diazinon.

### Fleas
These are certainly well-known pests to dog or cat owners. They may fall off a pet and wait in the lawn for another host animal. The insecticides diazinon, malathion, and Sevin are good controls.

# Occasional pests

Some of the insects and other pests included in this group can, in specific situations, cause extensive damage. But they are not nearly so common as sod webworm, grubs, and chinch bugs. Several are problems only in relatively confined regions. Others, such as wireworms, sowbugs, pillbugs, millipedes, and centipedes are widespread but rarely cause serious damage.

3x actual size

### Aphids
Frequently found in lawns. Recently, their damage has been on the increase. In areas of heavy infestation, treat with diazinon.

1⅓ x actual size

3x actual size

½ x actual size

### Sowbugs and pillbugs
These bugs are very similar in appearance and behavior, but pillbugs are the ones that can roll themselves into a ball. Usually they eat decaying organic matter. They are easily controlled by removing their cool, moist hiding places, such as leaves and organic debris.

### Wireworms
These larva of click beetles feed on lawn roots. They're brown, about one inch long. Only when present in excessive numbers will they damage lawns. Look for them as you would for grubs — in the root zone of the dead sections of grass. Control with diazinon.

### Snails and slugs
The silvery trails these pests leave behind are a giveaway to their presence. They'll be a lawn pest especially if a ground cover of vinca or ivy — a great hiding place for them — borders the lawn. Both are easily controlled with baits containing metaldehyde or Mesurol.

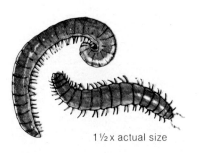

1½ x actual size

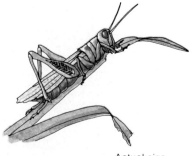

Actual size

Actual size

### Millipedes and centipedes
Rarely damaging to lawns, these segmented wormlike creatures are often found in or near them. Like sowbugs, they like cool, moist hiding spots. If there are too many in your yards, a good clean-up of trash or wood will control them.

### Grasshoppers
These insects will damage your lawn only if a great many move in at once. They are usually most abundant in late summer in more rural or suburban areas. Chemical control is rarely necessary, but Dursban is effective.

### Crickets
These won't eat much of your lawn but may be a problem especially as they try to move into your house for winter. Use diazinon granules or similar chemical control around the house if they become a problem.

# Lawn diseases and similar problems

As we mentioned in the section, "Insects and pests," diagnosing lawn problems can often be difficult, especially if considerable time has elapsed between the cause of the damage and the diagnosis. Many times the problem will be attributed to an insect or disease, when actually the climate, environmental conditions, or cultural practices are the cause. Mowing height, competition from tree roots, chlorosis, soil compaction, improper watering, and herbicide damage are some of the many factors that either cause the symptoms or are related to the development of the disease.

## The importance of proper lawn care

It is repeated again and again in this book that proper maintenance will reduce lawn problems. This is especially true when it comes to lawn disease. Most of the diseases that attack typical home lawns are due to improper management. Thatch is one of the most important factors that govern the frequency of disease in the home lawn. Thatch restricts the movement of air, water, and fertilizers into the soil, and generally weakens the lawn. This type of lawn is naturally much more disease prone.

When and how much you fertilize also has an important impact on dis-

ease development. An over-fertilized lawn, as well as an under-fertilized lawn, are more disease susceptible. Timing is also critical. For example, if you give a cool-season lawn heavy doses of growth-stimulating fertilizer in late spring and summer (periods of naturally slow growth), it becomes increasingly susceptible to leaf spot and *Fusarium* blight. It's important to follow a fertilizer program that conforms to the growth cycle of your particular lawn grass. The lawn experts say it best: "Let the grass grow, don't make it grow."

Watering practices also relate to disease frequency. Lawns that are watered deeply but infrequently usually have fewer disease problems. Constantly wet grass in poorly drained soil promotes disease.

Lawn diseases are easier to prevent than to cure. Follow these steps to prevent diseases from becoming established in your lawn.

✔Plant a grass type and variety that is adapted to your climate.

✔Mow at the proper height.

✔Fertilize at recommended rates and on a schedule that fits the growth cycle of your cool- or warm-season grass.

✔Water deeply and infrequently and only when the lawn needs it.

When a serious disease does attack your lawn despite adherence to these preventive measures, use of a chemical control is necessary.

## Fungicides

There are over a dozen chemicals commonly sprayed on lawns by homeowners to prevent and control disease. They are categorized as either "systemic" or "non-systemic."

Systemic fungicides work from inside the plant, so are usually the most effective. They are, however, very specific and will control only certain diseases.

Non-systemic fungicides work from outside the plant. They are best used before a disease starts. For example, if you know from past experience a certain disease will attack your lawn in two weeks or so, start spraying the appropriate fungicide now. This way the disease can be prevented.

Look at the chart for a breakdown on the uses of the various fungicides. Use the succeeding pages to help identify and control any diseases that occur in your lawn. For the sake of simplification, chemical names rather than trade names are used to describe controls in the disease descriptions.

## Common fungicides

| Common Name/ Trade Name | Uses |
| --- | --- |
| anilazine/ Dyrene | Dollar spot and melting out, rust, snow mold. Non-systemic. |
| benomyl/ Benlate Tersan 1991 Cleary 3336 | Brown patch, dollar spot, *Fusarium* patch, *Fusarium* blight, powdery mildew, and stripe smut. Has systemic action. |
| captan/ Orthocide | Melting out, damping off, and stripe smut. Non-systemic, contact only. |
| chloroneb/ Tersan SP Demosan | *Pythium* blight, grey snow mold. Non-systemic. |
| chlorothalonil/ Daconil 2787 Bravo | Brown patch, dollar spot, *Fusarium* patch, melting out, and red thread. Non-systemic fungicide. |
| cycloheximide/ Acti-dione | Brown patch, dollar spot, leaf spot, melting out, powdery mildew, snow mold. Non-systemic. |
| diazoben/ Dexon | Damping off, *pythium* (grease spot). Non-systemic. |
| Ethazol Koban Truban | *Pythium*. Non-systemic. |
| folpet/ Phaltan | Melting out. Non-systemic, contact only. |
| mancozeb/ Dithane M-45 Fore | Red thread, rust, and melting out. Non-systemic. |
| maneb/ Dithane M-22 | Rust. Non-systemic. |
| oxycarboxin/ Plantvax | Rust. Non-systemic. |
| PCNB/ Terraclor | Brown patch. Melting out. Slight systemic activity. |
| thiabendazole/ Mertect 140F. | Brown patch, dollar spot, *Fusarium* patch, snow mold. Non-systemic. |
| thiophanate methyl/Topsin Spot Clean Fungo-50 | Brown patch, dollar spot, *Fusarium* blight, *Fusarium* patch, stripe smut. Systemic. |
| thiram/ Tersan 75 | Should be combined with other fungicide. |

## Disease trouble shooting

| Looking closely: | Cause |
| --- | --- |
| Fungus growth can be seen on the blade: | |
| Black, long streaks of powdery spores | Stripe smut |
| White and powdery | Powdery mildew |
| Red or orange, like a powder | Rust |
| Grey and easily rubbed off | Slime mold |
| Visible spots on leaves, actual fungus is not visible (just the results of fungus infection) | |
| Reddish brown to blue-black and circular or oval | Leaf spot (melting out) |
| Straw colored bands with a reddish brown border | Dollar spot |
| **Looking at the whole lawn** | **Cause** |
| The diseased area is circular: | |
| Present in late winter or early spring | Snow mold |
| Present in spring, summer, or fall | |
| One inch to four feet or more in diameter | |
| Mushrooms just inside or outside the circle | Fairy ring |
| No mushrooms | Brown patch |
| One to eight inches in diameter | |
| Small, with many throughout the lawn | Dollar spot |
| Only in full sun and with green centers (frog-eye) | *Fusarium* blight |
| In low areas and often in streaks | Pythium |
| The diseased area is irregular in shape: | |
| New lawn seedlings wilt and die | Damping-off |
| Mature lawn affected, spots on leaves | Melting-out (leaf spot) |
| Mature lawn affected, thin, no spots on leaves | Nematodes |

Note: Due to space limitations, not all lawn diseases will be in this chart; this is only a helpful guide.

# Common lawn diseases

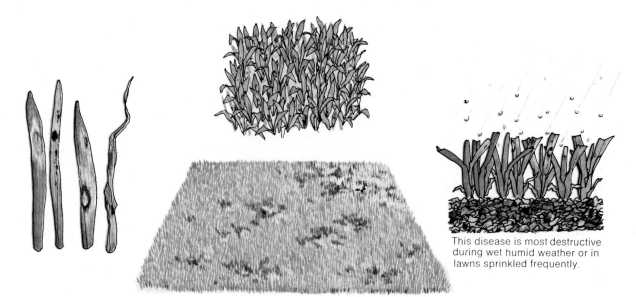

This disease is most destructive during wet humid weather or in lawns sprinkled frequently.

## Melting out, leaf spot:
### April to November

**Description:** Melting out refers to a number of leaf spot diseases favoring Kentucky bluegrass, fescue, and bermudagrass. The most obvious symptom of the disease is elongated circular spots on the leaves. These spots have a brown or straw-colored center with black to purplish borders.

**Favorable climatic conditions:** Cool, (50° to 70°F.) moist conditions are most favorable; first appears in the shade. Most severe in closely mowed lawns.

**Susceptible grasses:** 'Park' and 'Delta' Kentucky bluegrass are very susceptible.

**Resistant varieties:** 'Merion' and 'Adelphi' Kentucky bluegrass. Many of the newer improved bluegrass varieties also have good resistance.

**Cultural control:** Reduce shade. Improve aeration and water drainage. Mow at recommended height.

**Chemical control:** Anilazine, captan, chlorothalonil, cycloheximide, folpet, and mancozeb.

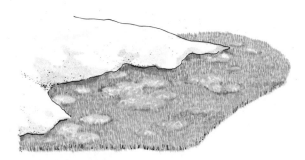

## Fusarium patch:
### September to May

**Description:** This disease is called pink snow mold if it develops under snow or at the margins of a melting snow bank. It causes circular patches 1 to 8 inches in diameter. Tiny white or pink masses are sometimes seen on dead leaves. Fungal threads, also white or pink, can be seen in early morning.

**Favorable climatic conditions:** Cool (40° to 60°F.) temperatures and moisture.

**Susceptible grasses:** Ryegrass, fescue, zoysiagrass, and colonial and creeping bentgrass.

**Resistant grasses:** Improved Kentucky bluegrass.

**Cultural control:** Reduce shade, if any. Improve soil aeration and drainage. Avoid excess nitrogen fertilization in the fall.

**Chemical control:** Benomyl, chlorothalonil, mancozeb, thiabendazole.

## Fusarium blight:
### May to October

**Description:** The disease begins as scattered light green patches ½ to 8 inches in diameter, that turn dull tan to reddish-brown. The most diagnostic of these larger diseased paches in the lawn is the "frog-eye" pattern. This is an apparently healthy green patch of grass partially or completely surrounded by a ring of dead grass.

**Favorable climatic conditions:** Hot, dry, and windy weather is especially favorable. It occurs most commonly in areas that have suffered water stress.

**Susceptible grasses:** Of the Kentucky bluegrasses, 'Arboretum,' 'Fylking,' 'Park,' and 'Dennstar.'

**Resistant varieties:** 'Glade,' 'Parade,' 'Sydsport,' 'Columbia,' 'Adelphi,' and Kentucky bluegrass.

**Cultural control:** Avoid heavy fertilization and follow correct watering and mowing practices. Light frequent watering will help during drought.

**Chemical control:** Benomyl and thiophanate have been most useful but control is difficult. Water the night before and thoroughly drench fungicide into turf.

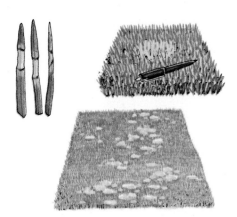

## Dollar spot:
### May to November

**Description:** A common fungus disease that attacks several different types of grass, but is most severe on bermuda and bentgrass. It kills in small spots from 3 inches to 12 inches in diameter, but the spots may coalesce into large areas. Diseased spots are usually bleached from tan to straw-colored.

**Favorable climatic conditions:** Moderate temperatures, excess moisture, and heavy thatch all contribute to this disease. Underfertilized lawns are more prone.

**Susceptible grasses:** Bentgrass, Kentucky bluegrass, bermudagrass, ryegrass, and fescues.

**Resistant varieties:** Some of the new, improved Kentucky bluegrasses.

**Cultural control:** Increase nitrogen, keep thatch at a minimum, water deeply when necessary.

**Chemical control:** Anilazine, benomyl, chlorothalonil, thiabendazole.

## Brown patch:
### July to August

**Description:** Recognize it by the large irregular, circular areas, which can be up to several feet in diameter. The patches usually have a brownish to grey discoloration, with a water-soaked appearance around the edges of the patch. Normally, only the leaves and stems are attacked.

**Favorable climatic conditions:** High temperatures (75° to 95°F), excessive thatch, high humidity, lush growth from over-fertilization, and excessive moisture are perfect for this disease.

**Susceptible grasses:** A serious disease in the South on centipede and St. Augustinegrass. It also attacks bentgrass, bermudagrass, dichondra, ryegrass, fescue and zoysiagrass.

**Resistant grasses:** Improved Kentucky bluegrass.

**Cultural control:** Avoid heavy nitrogen fertilization, reduce shading, and water deeply when necessary.

**Chemical control:** Benomyl, thiophonate, chlorothalonil.

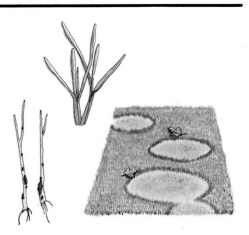

## Pythium, grease spot or cottony blight:
### July and August

**Description:** Generally a problem on newly established lawns but will occur on any lawn if conditions are favorable. The diseased area may be a few inches to several feet in diameter. It frequently occurs in small, circular spots about 2 inches across on closely cut lawns. Look for it in early morning while dew is still on the grass, or during humid weather. The diseased areas are surrounded by blackened blades covered with a white or grey fungus. Dry weather will stop the disease.

**Favorable climatic conditions:** High temperatures and excess moisture.

**Susceptible grasses:** Ryegrass, tall fescue, bentgrass, bermudagrass, and bluegrass.

**Resistant varieties:** None.

**Cultural control:** Avoid excessive watering during warm weather, don't overfertilize. Seed late in the fall.

**Chemical control:** Use a fungicide such a diazoben, mancozeb, koban or thiram at first sign of the disease.

## Damping off:
### Seedling lawns

**Description:** New seedings fail to fill in properly. If possible, look closely and you can see young seedlings have emerged from the soil, but collapsed. This disease is caused by a number of different fungal organisms.

**Favorable climatic conditions:** Overwatering after seeding especially if soil is heavy and days are overcast. No problem if starting from sprigs or stolons.

**Susceptible grasses.** Any seeded grass.

**Resistant varieties:** None.

**Cultural control:** Make sure pH is nearly neutral. Do not overwater and provide good drainage.

**Chemical control:** Use seeds treated with captan or thiram or spray captan or thiram at first sign of trouble.

## Powdery mildew:
### July to November

**Description:** First symptoms are light patches of dusty, white to light grey growth on grass blades. Lowest leaves may become completely covered. Generally not too serious a problem, but can be severe. Most common in shady areas.

**Favorable climatic conditions:** Slow or non-existant air circulation and shade are the most common causes.

**Susceptible grasses:** Kentucky bluegrass (especially 'Merion'), zoysia and bermudagrass.

**Resistant varieties:** 'Glade,' 'Nugget,' and 'Birka' Kentucky bluegrass; 'Fortress,' red fescue.

**Cultural control:** Reduce shade, if possible. Don't overwater. Avoid overfertilization.

**Chemical control:** Benomyl, cycloheximide.

## Rust:
### July to November

**Description:** This disease is appropriately named. The affected lawn will have a rust-colored cast noticeable from a distance. Close-up, the dustlike rust spores are in circular or long groups on grass leaves. The rust rarely causes severe damage to home lawns but are very serious where grasses are grown for seed.

**Favorable climatic conditions:** Moderately warm, moist weather. Dew that lasts on the lawn for 10 to 12 hours is enough to promote germination of the fungus spores. Any stress conditions which restrict growth of the lawn grass favors the development of rust.

**Susceptible grasses:** Most all commonly grown grasses can be affected by rust. Kentucky bluegrass and the ryegrasses are most frequently damaged.

**Resistant grasses:** Fine fescues.

**Cultural control:** Keep the lawn growing rapidly by fertilizing with nitrogen and frequent watering. Then, mow frequently, every four or five days.

**Chemical control:** Maneb, anilazine, and oxycarboxin are moderately effective.

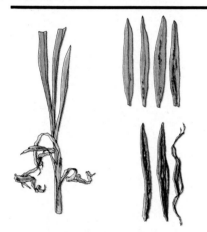

## Stripe smut:
### April to November

**Description:** Diseased plants are usually pale green and stunted. Long black stripes of spores are visible on the leaf blades. Affected leaves curl, die, and become shredded by the advancing disease.

**Favorable climatic conditions:** Moderate temperatures of spring and fall. Hot and dry weather will often halt the disease.

**Susceptible grasses:** Kentucky bluegrass and bentgrass are commonly attacked.

**Resistant grasses:** 'A-34,' 'Adelphi,' and 'Sydsport' are some of the many Kentucky bluegrasses that are resistant.

**Cultural control:** Keep thatch to a minimum and avoid overwatering.

**Chemical control:** Two systemics, benomyl and thiophanate will provide some control. Best applied in late fall.

## Typhula blight, grey snow mold:
### Any time with snow

**Description:** First appears as vaguely straw or tan-colored circular areas, a few inches to a few feet in diameter. The dead grass may actually be covered at some point with a greyish fungal growth. It occurs primarily in the northern United States and Canada, not reaching as far south as pink snow mold.

**Favorable climatic conditions:** A deep snow cover that is slow to melt.

**Suspectible grasses:** Most all the cool-season grasses.

**Resistant grasses:** None.

**Cultural control:** Be sure the lawn is not succulent or lush (overfertilized with nitrogen) before the first snowfall. Also, avoid excessive use of lime. Keep thatch layer to a minimum.

**Chemical control:** Apply anilazine or thiram in the fall before the first snowfall is forecast. Snow mold (pink and gray) is often only found in areas where snow lies for a long time, such as against a house or garage. These areas may be all that will need treatment.

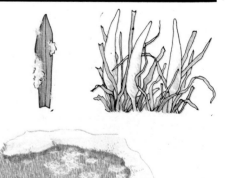

## *Corticium* red thread, pink patch:
### September to November

**Description:** This disease is most common to the Pacific Northwest, although it occasionally occurs in the northeast. The first symptoms are very small patches of dead grass. Under wet conditions, the fungus is visable as bright pink threads.

**Favorable climatic conditions:** Besides moist air, low levels of nitrogen favor the disease's development. When grass growth slows way down the disease becomes most prevalent.

**Susceptible grasses:** Red fescue, ryegrass, Kentucky bluegrass, and sometimes bentgrass.

**Tolerant grasses:** Many improved Kentucky bluegrass varieties.

**Cultural control:** Increased nitrogen.

**Chemical control:** Chlorothalonil, mancozeb.

## Ophiobolus patch:
### May to June, August to September

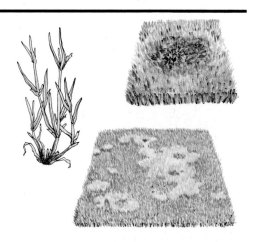

**Description:** Found only in the cool, moist, coastal regions of the Pacific Northwest. It first appears as small brown spots that will enlarge quickly with a favorable climate.

**Favorable climatic conditions:** Acid soils and maritime climate.

**Susceptible grasses:** Bentgrass is most commonly damaged but Kentucky bluegrass and ryegrass may also be bothered.

**Resistant grasses:** Fescues.

**Cultural control:** Best cultural control has been found with slightly acid soil. Apply 2 pounds of sulphur per 1,000 square feet when problem becomes severe.

**Chemical control:** Many recommend an acid-forming fertilizer, such as ammonium sulphate.

## Fairy ring:
### April to November

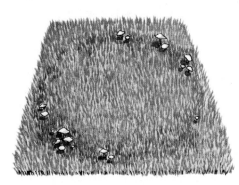

**Description:** Appears as a ring of dark green grass surrounding areas of dead or light-colored grass. The rings can be produced by the growth of any one of over 50 different kinds of fungus. The dying grass in the ring is caused by lack of water penetration.

**Favorable climatic conditions:** Fairy rings will develop in soils that contain undecomposed woody organic matter, such as dead tree roots or old construction materials. Primarily a problem in acid soils.

**Susceptible grasses:** All.

**Resistant grasses.** None.

**Cultural control:** Try to keep the lawn growing by applying adequate nitrogen fertilizer to hide the problem. Aerate the ring to improve water penetration. Keep areas wet for about two weeks, and mow frequently.

**Chemical control:** It's best to try to live with it. Complete eradication with a soil fumigant is difficult.

## Nematodes

**Description:** Nematodes are very common in the soil. These small worms are so small you need a microscope to see them, but scientists say they are the most common form of life on earth. There are thousands of different kinds, but only a few damage plants.

**Symptoms:** The grass will be generally unthrifty, thin, yellowish and drought susceptible in summer. It will not respond to other treatments such as aeration, fertilization, or watering. Upon inspection of the roots, they will be stubby, shallow, and possibly show swellings or galls. Complete diagnosis requires a microscope.

**Control:** Keep the grass as healthy as possible. If the presence of damaging nematodes is confirmed by a professional, consult with an experienced pest control operator or your County Extension Agent.

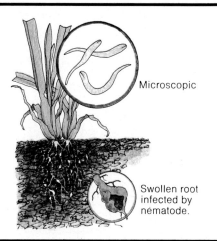

Microscopic

Swollen root infected by nematode.

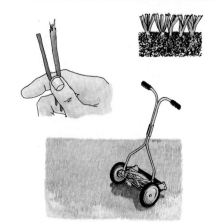

## Scalping and dull mower injury

Lawn scalping occurs whenever too much of the grass plant is cut off at one time. Reducing the height of the lawn by more than one-third creates a severe shock, but the results may not be immediately visible. When the mower blades dip down, suddenly removing most of the green part and the leaf blade of the lawn, the effects are obvious and should not be confused with insect or disease damage.

If your mower blades are dull, the lawn will have a greyish cast a day or so after mowing. This happens when the leaf tips have been shredded instead of cut, thus turning brown. This is especially noticeable when the weather is dry. Besides being unsightly, shredded tips are an easy entry point for many disease organisms.

## Chemical burn

Many lawns are damaged by spilled fertilizer, herbicide, gasoline, or by dog urination. These types of injuries are characterized by distinct and abrupt patches of dead grass. The damage of dog urination is slightly more confusing. It is characterized by bright green grass surrounding a patch of dead grass. The solution to these problems is to thoroughly drench the soil with water. If this doesn't work, you'll have to replace the soil under the dead spot and repatch the damaged area. (See page 56 for patching instructions.)

## Summer drying out

Drying out affects all grasses and can do considerable damage. It's easy to see but often mistaken for insect or disease damage. The soil could be compacted in one area or the sprinklers just missed a spot.

The first indication of insufficient water is when part of the lawn changes color from bright green to dull green. Then, if your footprints don't spring back in a reasonable length of time, water stress is confirmed.

If you have a cool-season grass, raise the cutting height at least one-half inch and water deeply. Check the soil moisture occasionally with a soil probe or moisture meter. If one area begins to show signs of drought, use a portable sprinkler or a hand held hose to soak the area. See the section on watering, pages 34 to 39.

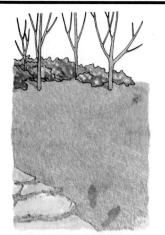

## Nitrogen or iron deficiency

Nitrogen is the nutrient needed by lawns in the greatest quantity. The actual amount will vary with the type of grass, but most need some lawn fertilizer every year. If you haven't been applying fertilizer, your lawn will probably be slightly yellow and not growing as well as it could.

If you have fertilized adequately and the lawn is still yellow and slow growing, the problem could be a lack of iron or improper pH. Some grasses, centipedegrass for instance, are especially sensitive to a lack of iron. A typical lawn fertilizer applied on a lawn that needs iron may actually increase the yellowish look. Apply iron either as a liquid spray or as a supplemental, granular, dry lawn application which is available in combination with nitrogen and sulfur.

# Growing lawns in the shade

The establishment and care of a good quality lawn in the shade is a real headache for many people. It need not be. Many beautiful lawns are grown in the shade of spreading trees. One of the measures of success is understanding the relationship between the tree and the grass underneath.

First of all, you must realize that there are many types of shade — light, half, dappled, full, and heavy. Few grasses will grow in full or heavy shade. Although it's difficult to figure out exactly, a lawn needs about 50 percent of the sunlight passing through a tree to sustain it underneath.

## Beating the competition

The grass growing underneath your trees is competing with the trees for water and nutrients, but most importantly, light. If left alone, and the shade is heavy enough, the tree will almost always win. The grass will become thin and spotty or gradually die out altogether.

Your job is to supply the requirements of the grass without harming the tree. Of course, if the tree is not a functional part of the landscape, you may decide to remove it in favor of the grass.

One of the first steps towards a successful lawn in the shade is to plant a shade-tolerant grass. Grasses are listed according to their ability to grow in shade on page 19. Even within species, certain varieties are more shade tolerant than others. The variety charts on pages 16 to 18 includes such strengths.

In areas of established turf, you may want to do small scale renovation and reseed with a better adapted grass. We also know of people who reseed every year with turf-type ryegrass to keep fresh new grass under trees.

The choice of grass may require some forethought. If you have recently planted a young tree, shade probably isn't a problem now, but may be in the future.

If you are considering planting trees in your lawn, plan ahead. Choose trees which cast filtered shade, and don't overplant. Several lawn trees are listed in the section, "Lawn tips," but if you really want to make an educated selection, see the Ortho book *The World of Trees.*

If a suitable grass is already growing under your trees, good maintenance practices will, of course, help the shaded lawn. However, there are some slight modifications of normal practices that will help even more.

Mow the lawn higher, at the highest cut suggested on page 51. More blade length means more light trapping ability. If fertilization is desired, consider soil injections for the tree instead of applying fertilizer directly on the lawn. A major problem of grass in the shade is overfertilization.

Watering deeply (but not overwatering) is especially important when trees are growing in the lawn. Shallow watering causes surface rooting which in turn causes mowing problems and allows the tree roots to rob the lawn of its nutrient needs.

If surface roots are already a problem, most trees can stand some root pruning without doing them much harm.

## Don't leave the leaves

Grasses growing in shade are more tender than those growing in full sun, so pay close attention to insect and disease problems.

Fallen leaves and heavy grass clippings can smother growing grass and increase damage from pests. This is particularly true in shaded areas.

## Too much shade

The most obvious, and sometimes the simplest solution to shade, is to prune the tree. Through proper thinning, as much as 40 percent of a tree's leaf surface can be removed without drastically changing the appearance of the tree. In fact, it usually enhances it.

Sometimes there are too many trees. Removal of a few can be helpful not only for the lawn, but for the trees that remain. Also, the Ortho book, *All About Ground Covers* lists many ground covers that do well in low light. You might also want to check into other alternatives such as an attractive stone or bark mulch.

*Don't give up on growing grass in the shade. Proper maintenance practices and adapted varieties make shade lawns possible in many situations. See text for more information.*

# Lawns in your area

These pages are really about climate, and the effects of climate on lawn growing. The length of growing season determines how much fertilizer your lawn will need each year. Summer rainfall patterns tell which lawns need irrigation systems or at least regular watering.

Obviously, winter low and summer high temperatures delineate to a great extent which grasses can be grown where.

In our earliest research, we questioned lawn owners around the country, who revealed a strong desire for specific information concerning the lawns in their climates. We heard comments like this one from Ohio:

"Most lawn books are limited by various geographical problems. I would like a book on growing lawns where I live." An individual from Texas said, "None of the books about lawns have much use around here."

## Diverse climates

The North is big and the grass climate in North Dakota is very different from New Jersey. Compare the climate of Minot, North Dakota, in the Plains

## NEW ENGLAND STATES

**Soil and climate.** Relatively moderate temperatures prevail throughout most of the region and make only occasional problems for lawn growing.

Rainfall is plentiful, rarely less than 30 inches in a year, but because of generally shallow soil, summer watering of lawns is usually necessary if they are to be kept green.

**Lime** is a must. Generally 50 to 200 pounds of ground limestone is necessary for every 1,000 square feet. A soil test will often recommend the appropriate quantity.

### Soil testing

Maine Soil Testing Service
25 Deering Hall
University of Maine
Orono, Maine 04473

University of New Hampshire
Analytical Services Department
Durham, New Hampshire 03824

Soil Testing Laboratory
Regulatory Services
University of Vermont
Burlington, Vermont 05401

Soil Testing Service
Department of Plant and Soil Sciences
Stockbridge Hall
University of Massachusetts
Amherst, Massachusetts 01003

Agronomy Section
College of Agriculture and
   Natural Resources
The University of Connecticut,
Storrs, Connecticut 06268

Rhode Island Soil Testing Service
District Office,
   Cooperative Extension Service
(check local telephone directory)

**Recommended grasses.** New England is solid Kentucky bluegrass territory. Fine fescues and a small percentage of turf-type ryegrass are often included in mixtures. For low-fertility lawns, mixtures of fine fescues and colonial bentgrass are well adapted.

### Publications offices

Cooperative Extension Service
University of Maine
Orono, Maine 04473
Out of state requests: Yes.

Cooperative Extension Service
Plant Science Department
Durham, New Hampshire 03824
Out of state requests: Yes.

The Extension Service
University of Vermont
Burlington, Vermont 05401
Out of state requests: Yes.

Cooperative Extension Service
Stockbridge Hall
University of Massachusetts
Amherst, Massachusetts 01003
Out of state requests: Yes.

Agricultural Publications
The University of Connecticut
Storrs, Connecticut 06268
Out of state requests: Yes.

Resource Information Office
24 Woodward Hall
University of Rhode Island
Kingston, Rhode Island 02881
Out of state requests: Yes.

## NEW YORK

**Soil and climate.** New York's climate, like most of the New England states, is humid and temperate. The quantity of rain is usually around 40 inches a year, most of which comes in summer. But it is not unusual for summer periods of high temperatures to coincide with short droughts. Lawns not watered during these times will suffer.

Throughout most of New York, the quantity of available sunshine is enough for excellent growth of grasses. During summer, about 60 percent of total possible sunlight is available. The growing season length varies from as few as a 100 to 180 days.

Most soil of the Northeast was developed under a natural forest cover. Most all of New York was also covered by glaciers.

The topography is characterized by long ridges of low mountains and hills that extend in a northeasterly direction.

**Lime** is frequently necessary. If pH tests below 6.0, use a soil test to determine exact needs. See pages 52 to 55.

**Soil testing.** Contact the Cooperative Extension Agent in your county, or:
Agronomy Department
804 Bradfield Hall
Cornell University
Ithaca, New York 14853

**Recommended grasses.** Kentucky bluegrass blends are the best lawngrass for New York. The red fescues are often mixed with Kentucky bluegrass for dry regions. Turf-type ryegrass is also frequently used in mixtures. Zoysiagrass is occasionally

grown in warmer areas of the state.

The major lawn pests are white grubs, chinch bugs, and sod webworm. (See pages 66 to 73.) The disease, melting out or leaf spot, caused by *Helminthosporium*, is the primary disease. It can be prevented by using the new improved varieties of Kentucky bluegrass which are tolerant of this disease (see page 16). Dollar spot, *Fusarium* blight, and stripe smut are disease problems in the southern part of the state.

### Publications office

Mailing Room
Building 7, Research Park
Cornell University
Ithaca, New York 14853
Out of state requests: Yes.

states to that of Atlantic City, New Jersey, in the Atlantic states. Minot receives an average of only 17 inches of rain per year. The average minimum temperature in January is −12°F. Only the hardiest of the cool-season grasses can be grown in this area. Quite a lot of watering is required to grow lawns in a climate this harsh, and winter damage to lawns is common.

Atlantic City, New Jersey, has a completely different set of climate circumstances. There they receive an average of 45 inches of rain per year and the average minimum temperature in January is 24°F. While this is still cool-season grass country, some areas of New Jersey and other southern Atlantic states can grow some of the hardier varieties of bermuda or zoysiagrass.

Local characteristics such as soil types and summer highs or winter lows, play an important role in which type of grass you grow and how you care for it. Knowing this kind of specific information will help you grow a better lawn.

## Extension information

The recommended grasses that are listed in the following were compiled from extension bulletins from each state. They are the result of years of research and experience and are one of the best guides to a beautiful lawn in your area.

At the end of each state or group of states are lists of addresses you can write to for additional local information. Most states produce high-quality pamphlets, brochures, or booklets that describe lawn growing. Don't hesitate to use these excellent resources.

The other addresses listed are for soil testing facilities. We've talked about the importance of soil tests throughout this book. In many cases the test is free, others may charge a nominal fee. Often, the most difficult part of getting your soil tested is knowing where to have it done.

| | TOTAL INCHES RAIN | INCHES JULY/AUG. | JULY % SUNSHINE | DEC. % SUNSHINE | JULY DAYS ABOVE 90°F. | AVERAGE MAXIMUM/MININUM TEMPERATURES | | | | | | | | | | | |
|---|---|---|---|---|---|---|---|---|---|---|---|---|---|---|---|---|---|
| | | | | | | JAN. | FEB. | MARCH | APRIL | MAY | JUNE | JULY | AUG. | SEPT. | OCT. | NOV. | DEC. |
| **NEW ENGLAND STATES** | | | | | | | | | | | | | | | | | |
| Bangor, ME | 44 | 10 | 62 | 48 | — | 28/12 | 32/14 | 38/22 | 52/34 | 64/44 | 72/52 | 78/58 | 77/56 | 68/49 | 57/39 | 46/31 | 32/17 |
| Caribou, ME | 36 | 7.7 | 60 | 40 | 1 | 20/1.5 | 23/2.7 | 33/14 | 45/28 | 60/39 | 70/49 | 76/54 | 73/51 | 65/43 | 53/35 | 38/25 | 24/8.2 |
| Grnville, ME | 43 | 10 | 60 | 48 | — | 24/4 | 29/7 | 35/14 | 49/28 | 63/38 | 72/48 | 78/52 | 75/50 | 66/43 | 54/34 | 41/25 | 27/10 |
| Portland, ME | 41 | 5.2 | 64 | 53 | 2 | 31/12 | 33/12 | 41/23 | 53/32 | 61/42 | 73/51 | 79/57 | 78/55 | 70/47 | 60/38 | 47/30 | 40/16 |
| Berlin, NH | 40 | 12 | 46 | 41 | — | 28/6 | 35/7 | 37/17 | 52/31 | 65/40 | 74/49 | 79/53 | 77/51 | 69/44 | 58/34 | 45/27 | 31/11 |
| Concord, NH | 36 | 6.0 | 62 | 47 | 5 | 31/10 | 34/11 | 42/22 | 58/32 | 69/41 | 78/52 | 83/57 | 80/54 | 72/46 | 62/36 | 48/28 | 35/15 |
| Brlngtn, VT | 33 | 7.2 | 65 | 33 | 3 | 26/8 | 28/9 | 38/20 | 53/33 | 60/43 | 76/54 | 81/58 | 78/56 | 70/49 | 59/39 | 44/30 | 30/15 |
| St. Jhnbry, VT | 38 | 10 | 52 | 38 | — | 29/7 | 34/11 | 40/19 | 56/32 | 69/42 | 78/51 | 82/55 | 80/53 | 72/47 | 60/36 | 46/28 | 32/13 |
| Boston, MA | 43 | 6.2 | 66 | 52 | 5 | 36/22 | 37/23 | 45/31 | 56/41 | 67/50 | 77/59 | 81/65 | 79/63 | 72/57 | 63/47 | 52/39 | 39/27 |
| Milton, MA | 47 | 6.8 | 57 | 46 | 2 | 34/19 | 35/19 | 43/27 | 56/37 | 67/46 | 75/56 | 80/62 | 79/60 | 71/53 | 62/44 | 50/35 | 37/22 |
| Wrchstr, MA | 45 | 7.8 | 62 | 50 | 1 | 31/16 | 33/17 | 41/25 | 55/36 | 66/45 | 75/55 | 79/61 | 77/59 | 70/52 | 61/42 | 47/32 | 34/20 |
| Brdgprt, CT | 39 | 7.2 | 62 | 52 | 3 | 37/23 | 38/24 | 45/31 | 56/40 | 67/50 | 76/60 | 81/66 | 80/65 | 74/58 | 65/48 | 53/39 | 40/27 |
| Hartford, CT | 43 | 7.3 | 62 | 48 | 8 | 34/16 | 36/18 | 47/27 | 59/36 | 70/46 | 79/56 | 84/61 | 82/59 | 74/51 | 64/41 | 51/32 | 37/20 |
| Provdnce, RI | 43 | 6.7 | 60 | 51 | 3 | 36/21 | 38/21 | 45/29 | 57/38 | 67/47 | 76/56 | 81/63 | 80/61 | 73/54 | 64/43 | 52/35 | 40/23 |
| **NEW YORK** | | | | | | | | | | | | | | | | | |
| Albany | 33 | 6.0 | 63 | 38 | 4 | 30/12 | 33/14 | 43/24 | 58/36 | 70/46 | 79/56 | 84/60 | 81/58 | 74/50 | 63/40 | 48/31 | 34/18 |
| Binghamton | 37 | 7.4 | 65 | 27 | 1 | 29/15 | 30/15 | 39/24 | 54/35 | 65/45 | 74/55 | 78/60 | 77/58 | 69/57 | 59/41 | 44/32 | 31/19 |
| Buffalo | 36 | 6.5 | 69 | 27 | 1 | 30/18 | 31/18 | 39/25 | 53/36 | 64/46 | 75/56 | 79/61 | 78/59 | 71/52 | 60/43 | 46/33 | 34/22 |
| Central Park | 40 | 7.7 | 65 | 49 | 6 | 38/26 | 40/26 | 48/34 | 61/43 | 71/53 | 80/63 | 85/68 | 83/66 | 77/60 | 67/51 | 54/41 | 41/29 |
| Elmira | 37 | 6.7 | 60 | 40 | 6 | 22/4 | 35/15 | 50/26 | 59/33 | 73/39 | 73/48 | 82/56 | 80/56 | 72/53 | 59/37 | 50/37 | 35/19 |
| Ithaca | 35 | 7.2 | 62 | 35 | 2 | 21/5 | 31/16 | 47/29 | 57/35 | 71/44 | 71/51 | 79/58 | 77/57 | 70/52 | 56/37 | 49/36 | 34/20 |
| Jamestown | 53 | 1.5 | 65 | 30 | 2 | 19/0 | 32/13 | 49/25 | 58/32 | 73/39 | 72/45 | 81/54 | 76/51 | 71/49 | 58/35 | 48/35 | 33/19 |
| Rochester | 31 | 5.8 | 69 | 31 | 4 | 31/17 | 33/17 | 41/25 | 56/36 | 67/46 | 78/56 | 82/60 | 80/58 | 73/51 | 62/42 | 48/33 | 35/22 |
| Syracuse | 36 | 6.6 | 65 | 25 | 3 | 31/16 | 33/16 | 41/25 | 56/36 | 68/46 | 78/56 | 82/61 | 80/59 | 73/52 | 62/42 | 48/34 | 35/21 |
| Utica | 49 | 7.4 | 63 | 32 | 5 | 19/6 | 28/16 | 45/30 | 59/33 | 76/44 | 75/51 | 83/58 | 80/57 | 70/53 | 59/38 | 49/34 | 33/18 |

## ATLANTIC and TRANSITIONAL STATES

**Soil and climate.** This is a large, diverse area, complex because it is transitional. It includes the states of New Jersey, Delaware, Maryland, West Virginia, and Kentucky, and stretches over 600 miles east to west from Atlantic City on the coast, to Louisville, Kentucky.

In the western foothills of the Appalachian Mountains, Elkins and Beckley have cool summers. Baltimore and Washington typify the hot summer areas. Rainfall is plentiful. It averages around 45 inches on the coast, decreasing towards the west and north.

Soils are of different types; many are very good. Before planting, make sure soil structure is good. Add organic matter, if necessary, and then check the pH level. Some soil within this area is very acid, (pH of 4.5 or more), while some is alkaline.

**Lime** will be necessary in some areas. Adjust pH as per soil test recommendations.

### Soil testing

University of Maryland
Soil Testing Laboratory
College Park, Maryland 20742

Soil Testing Laboratory
Cook College
Rutgers University
New Brunswick, New Jersey 08903

United States Department of Agriculture
Beltsville, Maryland 20705
(for Washington, D.C. residents)

Soil Testing Laboratory
University of Delaware
Newark, Delaware 19711

Soil Testing Laboratory
West Virginia University
Morgantown, West Virginia 26506

Soil Testing Laboratory
University of Kentucky
Lexington, Kentucky 40506

**Recommended grasses.** The cool-season grasses are by far the most common with tall fescue, a transition zone grass. Some of the hardy, warm-season grasses are also quite common.

A recommended cool-season lawn throughout the region is Kentucky bluegrass, or a mixture of Kentucky bluegrass, fine fescue, and turf-type ryegrass. Depending on local conditions and soil types, proportions of each will vary.

If you are growing Kentucky bluegrass in a transition area where it is not really well adapted, here's what to do:
1) Set your mower as high as possible during summer. Don't mow lower than 2 inches. 2) Fertilize in early spring and again in fall as weather cools — but never in summer. Stimulating new succulent growth during hot weather invites disease. 3) Water in the morning and make sure the soil is getting wet to at least 6 inches. Proper watering will help avoid many problems. 4) Use disease-resistant varieties such as 'Adelphi' and 'Majestic' in mixtures with other bluegrasses, fine fescues, and turf-type ryegrass. The other grasses will slow the spread of any disease. Good mixtures are available as seed or sod. 5) Dethatch every two or three years. A thick layer of thatch prevents air and water from reaching the roots and generally weakens the lawn. If attention to detail is not your style, consider another kind of grass.

Where higher summer temperatures and disease problems make growing the perfect lawn a full time job, consider tall fescue. 'Kentucky 31,' one of the most recommended varieties, originated from seed collected from William Suiter's farm in Menifee County, Kentucky. It makes a nice, tough though coarse-textured lawn.

Bermudagrass is sometimes used in southern and central New Jersey, southern Maryland, and in Delaware. 'Emerald' zoysiagrass can be grown throughout the region. It's used in Baltimore, parts of Sussex County, Delaware, and is widely used along the south shore of New Jersey. Zoysiagrass is less useful across the Appalachians; the growing season is often too short.

### Publications offices

Agricultural Duplication Services
University of Maryland
College Park, Maryland 20742
Out of state requests: Yes.

Mailing Room
Agricultural Hall
University of Delaware
Newark, Delaware 19711
Out of state requests: Yes.

United States Department of Agriculure
Beltsville, Maryland 20705
(for Washington, D.C. residents)

Publications Distributions Center
Cook College, Dudley Road
Rutgers University
New Brunswick, New Jersey 08903
Out of state requests: No.

Mailing Room
Communications Building
Evansdale Campus
West Virginia University
Morgantown, West Virginia 26506
Out of state requests: No.

Bulletin Room
Experiment Station Building
University of Kentucky
Lexington, Kentucky 40506
Out of state requests: Limited quantities.

## PENNSYLVANIA

**Soil and climate.** The main geographic features of Pennsylvania are the Appalachian Mountains and somewhat lower Allegheny Mountains. The elevation changes and microclimates created by them are responsible for most climate distinctions. The city of Erie on the shore of Lake Erie and Wilkes-Barre in the Pocono Mountains are two of the consistently coldest cities of Pennsylvania. Summer rain is heavier in cities such as Philadelphia and Allentown, which are nearer the Atlantic Ocean.

Soil along the Allegheny Plateau is mostly stony and thin. This includes cities such as Clearfield, Greensburg, and Indiana. Soil of Harrisburg and Scranton is mostly clay. The pH level varies throughout the state and should be checked.

**Lime** is usually necessary in some quantity. Check with a soil test. Apply ground limestone in fall.

**Soil testing.** Check with your local County Extension agent or write:
School of Agriculture
Pennsylvania State University
University Park
Pennsylvania 16802

**Recommended grasses.** Kentucky bluegrass is the best adapted and most widely used lawngrass in Pennsylvania. Varieties tested in and recommended for the state are: 'Fylking,' 'Baron,' 'Adelphi,' 'Glade,' 'Bonnieblue,' and 'Victa.' Red fescue can be used in mixtures in the cooler regions of western and northern Pennsylvania, and especially where excessive shade is a problem. Tall fescue is a good, tough lawngrass for the transitional climates of Pittsburgh and Philadelphia.

**Publications office**

Agricultural Mailing Room
Agricultural Administration Building
University Park, Pennsylvania 16802
Out of state requests: No.

| | TOTAL INCHES RAIN | INCHES JULY/AUG. | JULY % SUNSHINE | DEC. % SUNSHINE | JULY DAYS ABOVE 90°F. | AVERAGE MAXIMUM/MINIMUM TEMPERATURES | | | | | | | | | | | |
|---|---|---|---|---|---|---|---|---|---|---|---|---|---|---|---|---|---|
| | | | | | | JAN. | FEB. | MARCH | APRIL | MAY | JUNE | JULY | AUG. | SEPT. | OCT. | NOV. | DEC. |

## ATLANTIC and TRANSITIONAL STATES

| | TOTAL INCHES RAIN | INCHES JULY/AUG. | JULY % SUNSHINE | DEC. % SUNSHINE | JULY DAYS ABOVE 90°F. | JAN. | FEB. | MARCH | APRIL | MAY | JUNE | JULY | AUG. | SEPT. | OCT. | NOV. | DEC. |
|---|---|---|---|---|---|---|---|---|---|---|---|---|---|---|---|---|---|
| Atlntc Cty, NJ | 45 | 9.3 | 60 | 43 | 5 | 41/24 | 43/25 | 51/31 | 62/41 | 72/51 | 81/60 | 85/65 | 83/64 | 77/57 | 67/46 | 56/36 | 44/26 |
| Newark, NJ | 41 | 8.3 | 65 | 50 | 8 | 38/24 | 40/25 | 49/32 | 61/42 | 72/52 | 81/62 | 86/67 | 84/65 | 77/59 | 67/48 | 54/38 | 41/27 |
| Trenton, NJ | 40 | 8.9 | 65 | 48 | 7 | 39/25 | 41/26 | 49/33 | 62/42 | 72/52 | 81/62 | 85/67 | 83/65 | 76/58 | 66/48 | 51/39 | 41/28 |
| Annapolis, MD | 39 | 8 | 66 | 51 | 18 | 31/15 | 48/27 | 61/40 | 71/48 | 79/57 | 82/61 | 90/69 | 78/67 | 82/62 | 68/46 | 57/40 | 45/26 |
| Baltmr, MD | 40 | 8.3 | 65 | 48 | 11 | 42/25 | 44/26 | 53/32 | 65/42 | 75/52 | 83/62 | 87/66 | 85/65 | 79/58 | 68/46 | 56/36 | 44/26 |
| Cmbrlnd, MD | 29 | 4.9 | 59 | 39 | 21 | 30/11 | 47/22 | 64/35 | 72/42 | 80/50 | 83/56 | 93/63 | 89/63 | 82/58 | 67/40 | 54/38 | 42/23 |
| Easton, MD | 38 | 9.3 | 65 | 52 | 18 | 33/16 | 48/28 | 62/41 | 71/47 | 79/55 | 81/60 | 90/67 | 88/67 | 83/61 | 66/49 | 57/44 | 45/30 |
| Frederick,MD | 36 | 6 | 65 | 50 | 17 | 31/13 | 47/24 | 62/38 | 71/45 | 81/55 | 82/60 | 91/67 | 87/67 | 82/62 | 66/46 | 54/42 | 42/26 |
| Hagrstn, MD | 36 | 7.4 | 60 | 40 | 15 | 28/8 | 45/22 | 60/34 | 69/42 | 80/53 | 81/53 | 89/61 | 85/61 | 80/59 | 64/44 | 53/39 | 39/25 |
| Hancock, MD | 36 | 6.7 | 60 | 39 | 11 | 27/9 | 42/22 | 59/32 | 68/39 | 78/49 | 78/55 | 87/62 | 82/62 | 76/57 | 61/41 | 51/40 | 38/23 |
| LaPlata, MD | 42 | 8.9 | 67 | 51 | 12 | 34/14 | 51/27 | 64/40 | 72/44 | 78/54 | 80/59 | 88/67 | 88/66 | 82/59 | 67/46 | 58/42 | 46/27 |
| Salisbury, MD | 44 | 7.2 | 68 | 53 | 17 | 31/16 | 46/24 | 59/39 | 69/43 | 76/52 | 80/59 | 90/69 | 86/68 | 82/64 | 67/48 | 60/45 | 48/31 |
| Brdgvl, DE | 43 | 10 | 65 | 51 | 18 | 33/15 | 48/26 | 61/40 | 72/45 | 78/53 | 81/59 | 90/67 | 89/66 | 81/61 | 67/46 | 58/43 | 47/29 |
| Dover, DE | 42 | 8.7 | 65 | 51 | 18 | 34/16 | 49/27 | 62/40 | 71/44 | 79/54 | 83/60 | 90/68 | 88/68 | 82/62 | 68/47 | 59/42 | 47/29 |
| Grgetown, DE | 40 | 4.7 | 67 | 53 | 15 | 32/13 | 46/25 | 59/38 | 69/43 | 76/52 | 80/58 | 89/64 | 88/65 | 81/61 | 65/45 | 58/42 | 46/27 |
| Lewes, DE | 38 | 5.3 | 66 | 52 | 9 | 33/15 | 47/27 | 59/39 | 67/45 | 76/52 | 79/59 | 86/67 | 87/67 | 79/62 | 64/47 | 58/43 | 46/29 |
| Middletwn, DE | 41 | 6 | 65 | 51 | 12 | 32/14 | 46/26 | 57/37 | 70/44 | 79/53 | 81/58 | 88/65 | 86/65 | 81/60 | 66/45 | 56/41 | 44/27 |
| Milford, DE | 38 | 5 | 65 | 53 | 22 | 33/14 | 49/26 | 63/40 | 71/44 | 80/53 | 82/58 | 92/66 | 89/66 | 82/61 | 67/47 | 59/43 | 47/28 |
| Newrk U., DE | 41 | 8.7 | 64 | 51 | 13 | 31/13 | 45/24 | 60/36 | 69/43 | 79/52 | 81/58 | 89/65 | 86/65 | 80/60 | 66/44 | 57/44 | 43/26 |
| Wlmngtn, DE | 40 | 8.3 | 64 | 50 | 7 | 40/24 | 42/25 | 51/32 | 63/41 | 73/52 | 82/61 | 85/66 | 84/64 | 78/58 | 68/46 | 55/36 | 43/26 |
| Wshngtn, DC | 39 | 8.8 | 63 | 47 | 13 | 43/28 | 46/29 | 55/35 | 67/46 | 78/56 | 85/65 | 88/69 | 87/68 | 80/61 | 70/50 | 57/39 | 45/29 |
| Beckley, WV | 43 | 8.1 | 59 | 40 | 0 | 40/23 | 42/23 | 50/30 | 62/41 | 69/48 | 78/57 | 80/60 | 79/59 | 73/52 | 64/42 | 51/32 | 41/24 |
| Charlestn, WV | 41 | 8.1 | 60 | 39 | 7 | 44/25 | 46/27 | 55/34 | 68/44 | 77/52 | 83/61 | 86/64 | 84/63 | 79/56 | 69/45 | 56/35 | 45/27 |
| Elkins, WV | 43 | 9.0 | 59 | 40 | 1 | 41/19 | 42/20 | 51/27 | 63/37 | 71/45 | 78/53 | 80/57 | 79/55 | 74/49 | 65/38 | 52/29 | 42/21 |
| Hntngtn, WV | 39 | 7.5 | 60 | 39 | 7 | 43/26 | 45/27 | 55/34 | 67/44 | 76/53 | 83/61 | 86/65 | 85/63 | 79/56 | 69/45 | 55/36 | 45/27 |
| Prksbrg, WV | 38 | 7.6 | 62 | 29 | 8 | 41/24 | 44/26 | 53/33 | 66/43 | 75/52 | 83/61 | 86/65 | 85/63 | 79/56 | 68/45 | 54/36 | 43/27 |
| Lxngtn, KY | 44 | 8.2 | 70 | 42 | 6 | 41/24 | 44/26 | 53/34 | 66/45 | 75/54 | 83/62 | 86/66 | 85/64 | 80/58 | 69/47 | 54/35 | 44/27 |
| Louisvle, KY | 43 | 6.7 | 66 | 40 | 9 | 42/24 | 45/26 | 54/34 | 67/45 | 76/54 | 84/63 | 87/66 | 87/65 | 80/58 | 70/46 | 55/35 | 44/27 |

## PENNSYLVANIA

| | TOTAL INCHES RAIN | INCHES JULY/AUG. | JULY % SUNSHINE | DEC. % SUNSHINE | JULY DAYS ABOVE 90°F. | JAN. | FEB. | MARCH | APRIL | MAY | JUNE | JULY | AUG. | SEPT. | OCT. | NOV. | DEC. |
|---|---|---|---|---|---|---|---|---|---|---|---|---|---|---|---|---|---|
| Allentown | 42 | 8.5 | 60 | 39 | 7 | 36/20 | 38/21 | 48/28 | 61/38 | 72/48 | 81/58 | 85/63 | 83/61 | 76/53 | 66/42 | 52/33 | 39/23 |
| Erie | 38 | 6.9 | 63 | 30 | 0 | 32/18 | 32/18 | 40/25 | 53/36 | 64/45 | 73/56 | 77/60 | 76/59 | 70/53 | 60/43 | 46/34 | 35/23 |
| Harrisburg | 36 | 6.9 | 68 | 44 | 9 | 38/22 | 40/24 | 51/31 | 64/41 | 74/52 | 83/61 | 87/65 | 85/63 | 78/56 | 67/45 | 53/35 | 40/25 |
| Philadelphia | 40 | 8.2 | 63 | 49 | 7 | 40/24 | 42/25 | 51/32 | 63/42 | 74/52 | 83/62 | 87/67 | 85/65 | 78/58 | 68/47 | 55/37 | 43/27 |
| Cty. of Ptsbrgh | 36 | 6.9 | 53 | 23 | 6 | 37/24 | 39/24 | 49/32 | 62/42 | 72/52 | 81/61 | 84/65 | 83/63 | 77/56 | 66/45 | 52/36 | 40/27 |
| Gtr. Ptsbrgh | 36 | 7.0 | 60 | 30 | 3 | 35/21 | 37/21 | 47/29 | 61/39 | 71/49 | 79/58 | 82/61 | 81/59 | 75/53 | 64/42 | 49/33 | 37/24 |
| Wilkes Barre | 35 | 7.3 | 61 | 35 | 3 | 33/18 | 35/19 | 45/27 | 59/38 | 70/48 | 79/57 | 83/61 | 81/59 | 74/52 | 63/42 | 49/33 | 36/22 |
| Williamsport | 40 | 7.6 | 59 | 38 | 6 | 35/19 | 37/20 | 47/28 | 61/38 | 72/48 | 81/57 | 84/61 | 82/59 | 75/53 | 64/42 | 50/33 | 38/23 |

# OHIO

**Soil and climate.** Ohio is the most eastern of the lake states. As such, its climate is similar to the neighboring states of Illinois, and Indiana. Temperatures during the summer are high. Most climate variation is determined by latitude.

Topographically, northwestern Ohio is flat while the southeast is hilly. This is because the northwest was previously covered by a lake that was much higher than Lake Erie. Probably the best soil in the state is in this northwestern section.

More specifically, along the southeast through Portsmith, Wheeling, and as far north as Youngstown, the soil tends to be stony and thin. North central soil is also stony but depth is more variable. The average statewide pH is 6.3, and around Toledo the pH averages about 6.5. These are near ideal conditions for Kentucky bluegrass.

**Lime** may be necessary, but the best advice is to not use lime unless need is indicated by a soil test.

**Soil testing**
Cooperative Extension Office
Ohio State University
2120 Fyffe Road
Columbus, Ohio 43210

**Recommended grasses.** The most used Ohio lawngrass is Kentucky bluegrass. For seeding, use a blend of improved varieties such as 'Fylking,' 'Adelphi,' 'Baron,' or 'Sydsport.'

Use fine fescues only in shaded, low maintenance areas, or in a mixture with Kentucky bluegrass.

**Publications office**

Extension Office of Information
Ohio State University
2120 Fyffe Road
Columbus, Ohio 43210
Out of state requests: Yes.

# INDIANA

**Soil and climate.** Indiana's climate is largely continental with no large bodies of water (except in the extreme northwest) to moderate it. The northern half of the state is mostly level prairie but the south has many hills that contribute to a varying climate, even within short distances.

Generally, both temperatures and rainfall increase towards the south. The longest season is in the Evansville area. The shortest season in the west is in the Kankakee Valley area. Angola, Auburn, and Garrett have the shortest season in the northeast.

**Lime.** About a third of new lawns in Indiana need lime. Don't apply it unless pH has been checked and found to be lower than 6.0.

**Soil testing**
Plant and Soil Analysis Laboratory
Life Science Building
Purdue University
West Lafayette, Indiana 47907

**Recommended grasses.** Indiana is prime Kentucky bluegrass country, except for areas in the extreme south. Some of the newest improved varieties for Indiana are 'A-20' (available as sod), 'Adelphi,' 'Baron,' 'Victa,' 'Bonnieblue,' 'Glade,' and Nuggett.' Use a blend for an all-Kentucky bluegrass lawn or a mixture containing fine fescues and elite perennial ryegrasses.

In the south, around Evansville, homeowners can plant tall fescue or even bermuda or zoysiagrass.

**Publications office**

Mailing Room
Agricultural Administration Building
Purdue University
West Lafayette, Indiana 47907
Out of state requests: Yes.

# ILLINOIS

**Soil and climate.** The range of climates in Illinois is wide due to the state's north to south length. Climatologists have divided the state into three regions, all with a continental-type climate. The northern third has the coldest winters with warm summers; it extends as far south as Kankakee. The middle third stretches from Kankakee to Effingham. There, winters become progressively warmer towards the southern latitudes. The lowest third includes the rest of the state, from Effingham to Cairo.

In the north, the growing season averages 150 days. In Cairo the frost-free growing season is 200 days or more.

The northern two-thirds of Illinois soil is prairie. Prairie soil usually has a very dark brown or dark greyish brown surface. It is deep and fertile, developed primarily from native grass vegetation.

**Lime** is often needed especially in the southern part of the state. There, lime should be applied frequently. Before establishing a lawn, check the pH and add necessary limestone.

**Soil testing.** Soil testing is not offered by any public agency in Illinois. Check the telephone directory for private laboratories.

**Recommended grasses.** Kentucky bluegrass is the best lawngrass for most of Illinois. (Check the variety list on page 16.) It is often mixed with red fescue or turf-type ryegrass, both of which enhance establishment vigor and mix well.

Tall fescue, planted alone, is a good, tough, play lawn for central and southern Illinois, although it may be injured during the coldest winters.

**Publications office**
University of Illinois
Agricultural Publications Office
123 Mumford Hall
Urbana, Illinois 61801
Out of state requests: No.

# IOWA

**Soil and climate:** Iowa's climate is a continental type. That means most rain falls during the warm period of April to September. During the summer, periods of drought accompanied by hot winds will damage a lawn unless it is watered frequently. Northwood, near the Minnesota border, usually receives the heaviest snowfall. Bonapart at the Missouri border receives the least.

**Lime** is often lacking, especially for soils where lawns have not been grown before. Check pH with a soil test.

**Soil testing**
Soil Testing Laboratory
Cooperative Extension Service
Iowa State University
Ames, Iowa 50010

**Recommended grasses.** Kentucky bluegrass is the dominant lawngrass of Iowa as elsewhere in this climate. Common Kentucky bluegrass is acceptable in some situations, but the improved or elite types will not only provide greater beauty and utility, but also improved disease resistance. Turf-type ryegrass may be a mix component. Tall fescues are coarse bladed but make a good, tough, play lawn.

**Publications office**
Bulletin Room
Cooperative Extension Service
Iowa State University
Ames, Iowa 50010
Out of state requests: Yes.

| | TOTAL INCHES RAIN | INCHES JULY/AUG. | JULY % SUNSHINE | DEC. % SUNSHINE | JULY DAYS ABOVE 90°F. | AVERAGE MAXIMUM/MININUM TEMPERATURES | | | | | | | | | | | |
| | | | | | | JAN. | FEB. | MARCH | APRIL | MAY | JUNE | JULY | AUG. | SEPT. | OCT. | NOV. | DEC. |
|---|---|---|---|---|---|---|---|---|---|---|---|---|---|---|---|---|---|
| **OHIO** | | | | | | | | | | | | | | | | | |
| Akron | 35 | 6.5 | 62 | 31 | 11 | 39/12 | 36/19 | 45/27 | 59/38 | 70/47 | 79/57 | 83/61 | 84/59 | 75/53 | 69/43 | 49/33 | 41/22 |
| Cincinnati | 40 | 7.0 | 68 | 38 | 10 | 40/24 | 43/26 | 52/33 | 65/45 | 75/54 | 84/62 | 87/66 | 86/64 | 80/57 | 69/47 | 53/36 | 42/27 |
| Cleveland | 35 | 6.4 | 68 | 26 | 3 | 33/20 | 35/21 | 44/28 | 58/38 | 68/48 | 78/57 | 82/61 | 80/60 | 74/53 | 64/44 | 49/34 | 36/24 |
| Columbus | 37 | 7.1 | 63 | 31 | 6 | 36/20 | 39/21 | 49/29 | 63/39 | 73/49 | 82/59 | 85/62 | 84/60 | 78/53 | 66/42 | 51/32 | 39/23 |
| Dayton | 34 | 6.1 | 68 | 37 | 7 | 36/20 | 39/22 | 48/30 | 62/41 | 72/51 | 82/61 | 85/64 | 83/63 | 77/55 | 66/45 | 50/33 | 38/23 |
| Mansfield | 34 | 6.4 | 65 | 32 | 4 | 35/21 | 38/22 | 47/29 | 60/40 | 70/50 | 80/59 | 84/63 | 82/62 | 76/55 | 65/44 | 50/34 | 38/24 |
| Toledo | 31 | 6.3 | 68 | 34 | 5 | 32/17 | 35/19 | 45/27 | 59/37 | 70/47 | 80/57 | 84/61 | 82/59 | 76/52 | 65/41 | 48/31 | 35/20 |
| Youngstown | 38 | 7.1 | 64 | 31 | 3 | 33/18 | 35/19 | 44/26 | 58/37 | 69/46 | 78/56 | 82/60 | 80/58 | 74/51 | 63/42 | 48/33 | 36/22 |
| **INDIANA** | | | | | | | | | | | | | | | | | |
| Evansville | 42 | 6.7 | 76 | 41 | 15 | 41/24 | 45/26 | 55/34 | 68/45 | 77/54 | 86/64 | 89/67 | 88/64 | 81/57 | 71/45 | 55/34 | 44/26 |
| Fort Wayne | 36 | 6.8 | 73 | 37 | 5 | 33/18 | 35/20 | 45/28 | 59/39 | 70/49 | 80/59 | 84/62 | 82/60 | 76/53 | 65/42 | 48/32 | 36/21 |
| Indianapolis | 39 | 6.5 | 70 | 40 | 6 | 36/20 | 39/22 | 49/30 | 63/42 | 73/51 | 82/61 | 85/64 | 84/62 | 78/55 | 67/44 | 50/33 | 39/23 |
| Lafayette | 37 | 11 | 70 | 43 | 14 | 17/-3 | 34/17 | 54/34 | 67/44 | 81/56 | 79/58 | 89/64 | 80/61 | 77/56 | 61/40 | 49/35 | 32/16 |
| Muncie | 38 | 6.8 | 68 | 43 | 19 | 18/-1 | 37/22 | 56/38 | 68/45 | 81/57 | 82/62 | 90/70 | 82/65 | 78/59 | 63/43 | 51/38 | 36/21 |
| Oolitic | 45 | 7.6 | 70 | 44 | 13 | 21/0 | 39/18 | 59/34 | 69/43 | 80/54 | 81/58 | 88/65 | 83/62 | 80/57 | 64/38 | 53/37 | 37/19 |
| South Bend | 36 | 6.9 | 72 | 37 | 4 | 31/16 | 34/18 | 44/27 | 58/38 | 69/47 | 79/58 | 83/62 | 82/60 | 75/53 | 64/43 | 47/32 | 35/21 |
| Terra Haute | 38 | 6.4 | 71 | 46 | 17 | 19/0 | 37/17 | 57/35 | 68/43 | 82/57 | 83/59 | 91/66 | 84/64 | 81/57 | 64/42 | 53/37 | 35/19 |
| **ILLINOIS** | | | | | | | | | | | | | | | | | |
| Cairo | 47 | 6.7 | 75 | 45 | 17 | 44/29 | 48/32 | 57/39 | 69/51 | 79/60 | 87/68 | 90/72 | 88/70 | 81/62 | 71/52 | 57/40 | 46/32 |
| Carbondale | 43 | 6.9 | 73 | 50 | 18 | 26/2 | 45/20 | 62/37 | 73/46 | 83/57 | 86/63 | 90/69 | 87/65 | 82/60 | 68/40 | 56/39 | 41/23 |
| Chicago | 34 | 7.2 | 70 | 38 | 9 | 31/17 | 35/20 | 45/29 | 59/40 | 70/50 | 81/60 | 84/65 | 83/64 | 76/56 | 65/46 | 48/33 | 35/22 |
| Decatur | 38 | 6.2 | 73 | 42 | 22 | 20/1 | 40/19 | 57/35 | 72/46 | 84/56 | 83/59 | 91/66 | 84/61 | 81/57 | 65/42 | 51/35 | 36/19 |
| Moline | 36 | 7.9 | 71 | 41 | 8 | 30/13 | 34/17 | 45/26 | 61/40 | 72/50 | 81/60 | 85/64 | 84/62 | 76/53 | 66/43 | 48/30 | 35/18 |
| Peoria | 35 | 6.8 | 69 | 40 | 7 | 32/16 | 36/19 | 46/28 | 62/41 | 72/51 | 82/61 | 85/65 | 84/63 | 76/55 | 66/44 | 49/31 | 36/20 |
| Rockford | 37 | 7.9 | 71 | 45 | 6 | 29/11 | 33/15 | 43/25 | 59/37 | 70/47 | 80/58 | 84/61 | 83/60 | 72/52 | 64/41 | 46/29 | 33/17 |
| Springfield | 35 | 8.5 | 73 | 42 | 10 | 35/19 | 39/22 | 49/30 | 61/43 | 74/53 | 83/62 | 87/66 | 85/64 | 79/56 | 68/45 | 51/33 | 38/23 |
| **IOWA** | | | | | | | | | | | | | | | | | |
| Burlington | 35 | 7.1 | 77 | 51 | 11 | 32/14 | 36/18 | 47/27 | 62/40 | 73/51 | 82/61 | 86/65 | 85/63 | 77/54 | 67/44 | 49/30 | 36/19 |
| Cedar Rapids | 36 | 7.3 | 71 | 49 | 11 | 17/-3 | 36/15 | 50/32 | 67/42 | 79/55 | 81/57 | 86/65 | 77/59 | 72/55 | 58/40 | 42/27 | 25/12 |
| Davenport | 36 | 7.9 | 71 | 41 | 11 | 18/1 | 37/19 | 53/35 | 69/47 | 81/60 | 82/61 | 88/68 | 80/62 | 75/58 | 61/44 | 47/32 | 30/15 |
| Des Moines | 31 | 6.6 | 72 | 45 | 10 | 27/11 | 32/16 | 42/25 | 60/39 | 71/51 | 80/61 | 85/65 | 83/63 | 75/54 | 65/44 | 46/29 | 33/17 |
| Dubuque | 40 | 8.3 | 70 | 46 | 4 | 26/9 | 30/13 | 41/23 | 58/37 | 68/47 | 78/57 | 82/61 | 81/60 | 72/51 | 62/41 | 44/27 | 31/15 |
| Ottumwa | 37 | 8.3 | 72 | 50 | 15 | 19/1 | 38/19 | 53/36 | 69/47 | 79/60 | 84/62 | 91/68 | 80/62 | 75/58 | 61/43 | 47/31 | 30/16 |
| Sioux City | 26 | 6.2 | 76 | 51 | 10 | 28/8 | 33/13 | 43/23 | 61/37 | 72/49 | 81/59 | 87/64 | 85/62 | 75/51 | 66/40 | 47/26 | 33/14 |
| Waterloo | 38 | 8.2 | 71 | 48 | 6 | 26/7 | 30/11 | 41/22 | 58/36 | 70/47 | 79/58 | 84/61 | 82/59 | 73/50 | 63/40 | 45/26 | 31/13 |

## NORTH AND SOUTH DAKOTA

**Soil and climate.** The climate of the Dakotas can be semi-arid and given to wide and rapid temperature fluctuation. Average rainfall is around 30 inches a year. The rain may fall gently, or as heavy cloudbursts. Some areas in western sections generally receive no more than 10 to 15 inches of rain in a year.

The eastern edge of the Dakotas have a generally fertile loam soil, though it may vary in depth. To the west, soils are far more variable, from very good to very poor. **Lime** applications are rarely needed. A soil test will show need, if any, for lime as well as other characteristics of the soil.

**Soil testing**
Soil Testing Laboratory
Waldron Hall
North Dakota State University
Fargo, North Dakota 58102
Soil Testing Laboratory
South Dakota State University
Brookings, South Dakota 57007

**Recommended grasses.** The short, native grasses are the natural vegetation of the northern Great Plains. Blue grama, buffalograss, wheatgrass, and others are hardy and adapted to the dry, harsh climate.

Most home lawns, however, are Kentucky bluegrass and fine fescue mixtures.

**Publications offices**
Department of Agricultural Communications
North Dakota State University
Fargo, North Dakota 58102
Out of state requests: Yes.

Bulletin Room
South Dakota State University
Extension Building
Brookings, South Dakota 57007
Out of state requests: Yes.

## NEBRASKA

**Soil and climate.** Nebraska varies from the Dakotas by having a more mild climate: summers are longer and winters are less cold.

Like the Dakotas, soil is on the average, better towards the east. In many areas proper preparation of the soil before planting can be an important step towards establishment and maintenance of your lawn.
**Lime** applications are usually not necessary.
**Soil testing.** Check with your County

Extension Agent or write:
Soil Testing Laboratory
University of Nebraska-Lincoln
Department of Agronomy
Keim Hall, East Campus
Lincoln, Nebraska 68503
**Recommended grasses.** Kentucky bluegrass combined with the fine fescues make a good all-around Nebraska lawn. The turf-type ryegrasses are sometimes used. They have many advantages and mix well in a bluegrass-fescue lawn, but aren't quite as winter hardy.

Tall fescue, with winter hardiness roughly comparable to the ryegrasses, is also a favorite in southern Nebraska. Zoysia and bermudagrass are often grown south of the Platte in cities like Lincoln, Hastings, and McCook although they are at the northern limits of their range.
**Publications office**
University of Nebraska-Lincoln
Department of Agricultural Communications
Lincoln, Nebraska 68583
Out of state requests: Yes.

## MISSOURI

**Soil and climate.** The geography and climate of Missouri is divided into three separate regions. The northwest is prairie, extending into neighboring Kansas, Nebraska, and Iowa. Cities like St. Joseph or Independence in the northwest are often dry and have cold winters. Soil in these cities may be slightly alkaline.

Extending through the center of the state from the northeast to the southwest is the Ozark Plateau. Springfield and Rolla are located here. The Ozarks have less severe winters than the prairies, and cooler summers compared to the southeast.

Cape Girardeau, Sikeston, and Poplar

Bluff are cities in the southeast lowlands. Growing seasons are around 200 days and rain is plentiful — about 45 inches a year. Soil here is acid. Most areas are well drained but some are swampy.

**Lime** is very likely needed, especially in the southeast. Check by testing the soil.
**Soil testing**
Soil Testing Laboratory
University of Missouri
Columbia, Missouri 65201
**Recommended grasses.** Kentucky bluegrass, fine fescue, and turf-type ryegrass are the predominant cool-season grasses.

The highest quality lawns are usually a mixture of improved varieties of these three grasses.

'Meyer' zoysiagrass grows well in the southern, long growing-season areas. It requires plenty of heat and a good, long season for best growth.

Bermudagrass is often grown in the southern areas.
**Publications office**
Extension Publications
206 Whitten Hall
University of Missouri-Columbia
Columbia, Missouri 65201
Out of state requests: Yes.

## KANSAS

**Soil and climate.** Kansas is in the center of the United States. The slope of the land is gradual from the northwest to the southeast. This slope is apparent in measures of climate, too. The southeast — Independence, Parsonsville, Pittsburgh, Chanute — receives about twice the rain, has a longer growing season (by 40 or more days), and has warmer winters and summers compared to northwestern Kansas. The soil also varies. Kansas City soil is frequently acid as is soil in the above-named cities of southeastern Kansas.

Western Kansas is a part of the Great Plains. Here, wind erosion is a problem

and blowing soil may make new lawn establishment difficult. The climate is quite variable month to month and year to year. Humidity is low and evaporation is fast.

The soil is sandy or fairly heavy (called "hard lands"). Both are fairly high in nutrients.
**Lime** may be necessary in the east, especially the southeast. West Kansas rarely needs lime.
**Soil testing** is available through local County Extension offices or write:
Agronomy Department
Kansas State University
Manhattan, Kansas 66506

**Recommended grasses.** Cool-season grasses are generally used, but in the south and western sections of the state, bermudagrass and some of the native grasses, buffalograss or blue grama for instance, are useful. Buffalograss will form a "lawn" on less than 15 inches of rain a year. Buy treated buffalograss seed or establishment may be very slow and erratic.
**Publications office**
Publications Distribution Office
Umberget Hall
Kansas State University
Manhattan, Kansas 66506
Out of state requests: Yes.

| | TOTAL INCHES RAIN | INCHES JULY/AUG. | JULY % SUNSHINE | DEC. % SUNSHINE | JULY DAYS ABOVE 90°F. | AVERAGE MAXIMUM/MINIMUM TEMPERATURES | | | | | | | | | | | |
| --- | --- | --- | --- | --- | --- | --- | --- | --- | --- | --- | --- | --- | --- | --- | --- | --- | --- |
| | | | | | | JAN. | FEB. | MARCH | APRIL | MAY | JUNE | JULY | AUG. | SEPT. | OCT. | NOV. | DEC. |

## NORTH and SOUTH DAKOTA

| | | | | | | | | | | | | | | | | | |
| --- | --- | --- | --- | --- | --- | --- | --- | --- | --- | --- | --- | --- | --- | --- | --- | --- | --- |
| Bismark, ND | 16 | 4.2 | 76 | 47 | 8 | 19/-3 | 24/2 | 35/15 | 55/31 | 67/42 | 76/52 | 84/57 | 83/55 | 71/44 | 60/33 | 39/18 | 26/5 |
| Fargo, ND | 20 | 6.0 | 71 | 43 | 5 | 15/-4 | 21/1 | 33/15 | 53/32 | 67/42 | 76/53 | 83/59 | 82/57 | 70/46 | 58/35 | 37/20 | 22/4 |
| Minot, ND | 17 | 4.5 | 69 | 53 | 5 | 8/-12 | 31/12 | 43/19 | 63/33 | 77/50 | 76/52 | 83/56 | 74/47 | 64/46 | 58/34 | 36/15 | 14/-2 |
| Williston, ND | 14 | 3.6 | 75 | 47 | 8 | 19/-3 | 26/3 | 36/14 | 55/30 | 67/41 | 75/50 | 84/56 | 83/54 | 70/43 | 59/32 | 38/18 | 26/5 |
| Aberdeen, SD | 19 | 4.8 | 72 | 50 | 2 | 12/-9 | 35/13 | 42/25 | 66/38 | 77/52 | 80/55 | 81/53 | 79/52 | 71/48 | 59/34 | 36/18 | 18/4 |
| Pierre, SD | 18 | 4.4 | 73 | 55 | 9 | 18/-4 | 41/19 | 47/26 | 67/39 | 79/52 | 85/58 | 86/56 | 84/55 | 76/49 | 60/36 | 42/22 | 26/11 |
| Rpd City, SD | 17 | 3.6 | 72 | 54 | 11 | 34/10 | 38/14 | 43/20 | 51/32 | 67/43 | 76/52 | 86/59 | 86/57 | 75/46 | 64/36 | 47/23 | 38/15 |
| Sx Falls, SD | 25 | 5.8 | 74 | 51 | 12 | 25/4 | 30/9 | 40/20 | 58/34 | 70/46 | 79/56 | 85/61 | 84/60 | 73/49 | 63/38 | 43/23 | 30/10 |

## NEBRASKA

| | | | | | | | | | | | | | | | | | |
| --- | --- | --- | --- | --- | --- | --- | --- | --- | --- | --- | --- | --- | --- | --- | --- | --- | --- |
| Lincoln | 29 | 6.9 | 74 | 52 | 18 | 33/12 | 38/17 | 47/26 | 63/39 | 73/51 | 83/61 | 89/66 | 87/64 | 77/54 | 68/44 | 50/28 | 38/17 |
| North Platte | 20 | 5.0 | 74 | 60 | 12 | 37/10 | 41/15 | 47/21 | 61/34 | 71/45 | 81/55 | 88/61 | 87/59 | 77/48 | 67/35 | 50/22 | 40/14 |
| Omaha | 30 | 7.7 | 77 | 56 | 14 | 33/12 | 38/17 | 48/26 | 61/40 | 74/51 | 83/61 | 89/66 | 87/64 | 79/54 | 69/43 | 51/29 | 38/18 |
| Chadron | 16 | 3.1 | 73 | 60 | 17 | 30/3 | 48/23 | 49/23 | 64/38 | 74/48 | 86/58 | 90/61 | 81/55 | 80/49 | 65/36 | 46/24 | 35/13 |
| Grand Island | 23 | 5.5 | 78 | 60 | 18 | 29/6 | 49/19 | 53/29 | 68/45 | 77/57 | 85/62 | 91/67 | 82/61 | 77/54 | 65/40 | 50/29 | 41/15 |
| Sidney | 17 | 4.3 | 71 | 65 | 17 | 32/3 | 48/19 | 46/19 | 62/34 | 73/44 | 84/54 | 88/58 | 82/54 | 80/46 | 67/32 | 48/22 | 31/8 |
| Valentine | 18 | 4.9 | 75 | 59 | 16 | 30/4 | 49/21 | 46/24 | 65/40 | 76/52 | 86/59 | 90/62 | 83/55 | 79/50 | 65/39 | 48/28 | 37/16 |

## MISSOURI

| | | | | | | | | | | | | | | | | | |
| --- | --- | --- | --- | --- | --- | --- | --- | --- | --- | --- | --- | --- | --- | --- | --- | --- | --- |
| Columbia | 37 | 7.0 | 75 | 46 | 16 | 38/21 | 43/24 | 51/32 | 65/45 | 75/54 | 83/63 | 87/67 | 86/65 | 79/57 | 69/47 | 54/34 | 41/24 |
| Kansas City | 37 | 8.2 | 82 | 59 | 19 | 36/18 | 41/23 | 51/31 | 65/44 | 75/54 | 83/63 | 88/67 | 87/66 | 79/57 | 68/47 | 51/33 | 39/23 |
| Kirksville | 36 | 7.7 | 72 | 50 | 22 | 22/2 | 41/20 | 57/36 | 69/46 | 80/57 | 85/61 | 92/69 | 83/63 | 78/57 | 64/43 | 50/33 | 34/18 |
| Poplar Bluff | 45 | 6.0 | 74 | 51 | 23 | 30/10 | 49/24 | 64/40 | 75/50 | 84/60 | 89/66 | 91/70 | 90/68 | 82/62 | 70/44 | 61/43 | 43/24 |
| St. Joseph | 36 | 7.8 | 77 | 55 | 20 | 25/4 | 45/24 | 58/38 | 70/48 | 77/59 | 86/64 | 91/70 | 84/65 | 78/59 | 66/43 | 51/34 | 38/20 |
| St. Louis | 36 | 6.6 | 72 | 43 | 14 | 40/23 | 44/26 | 53/33 | 67/46 | 76/55 | 85/65 | 88/69 | 87/67 | 80/59 | 70/48 | 54/36 | 43/26 |
| Springfield | 40 | 6.6 | 72 | 49 | 16 | 43/23 | 47/26 | 55/33 | 68/45 | 76/54 | 84/63 | 89/66 | 89/65 | 81/57 | 71/47 | 56/34 | 46/26 |
| Vichy | 42 | 4.5 | 75 | 50 | 17 | 27/9 | 46/26 | 60/39 | 72/50 | 79/60 | 82/64 | 89/71 | 86/67 | 80/62 | 67/47 | 52/38 | 41/24 |

## KANSAS

| | | | | | | | | | | | | | | | | | |
| --- | --- | --- | --- | --- | --- | --- | --- | --- | --- | --- | --- | --- | --- | --- | --- | --- | --- |
| Chanute | 40 | 8.6 | 78 | 60 | 21 | 31/11 | 53/26 | 61/37 | 72/50 | 80/59 | 87/65 | 90/70 | 86/67 | 81/62 | 70/47 | 55/37 | 45/23 |
| Concordia | 28 | 6.4 | 80 | 61 | 21 | 29/9 | 51/24 | 59/34 | 68/46 | 79/57 | 86/64 | 93/69 | 84/64 | 80/58 | 67/44 | 52/31 | 41/18 |
| Dodge City | 21 | 5.7 | 79 | 65 | 22 | 43/19 | 47/23 | 54/28 | 67/41 | 76/52 | 86/61 | 91/67 | 90/65 | 81/56 | 71/45 | 55/30 | 45/22 |
| Goodland | 17 | 4.8 | 75 | 68 | 19 | 36/9 | 53/21 | 52/25 | 65/39 | 74/50 | 86/58 | 91/62 | 83/59 | 82/52 | 67/38 | 53/25 | 46/16 |
| Hill City | 24 | 6.2 | 77 | 63 | 22 | 35/10 | 55/21 | 59/29 | 70/44 | 80/55 | 91/62 | 94/68 | 87/63 | 83/54 | 70/41 | 54/28 | 45/17 |
| Salina | 28 | 6.4 | 80 | 63 | 24 | 32/11 | 53/25 | 61/36 | 69/47 | 79/59 | 87/66 | 94/71 | 86/66 | 81/61 | 69/46 | 53/34 | 44/20 |
| Topeka | 35 | 8.4 | 69 | 51 | 15 | 38/18 | 44/23 | 53/30 | 66/43 | 76/53 | 84/63 | 89/67 | 88/66 | 80/56 | 70/45 | 54/32 | 42/22 |
| Wichita | 31 | 7.4 | 74 | 58 | 21 | 41/21 | 47/25 | 55/32 | 68/45 | 77/55 | 86/65 | 92/70 | 91/68 | 82/59 | 71/48 | 56/34 | 44/25 |

## MICHIGAN

**Soil and climate.** Along the shorelines, climate is dominated by the lakes. Both spring and fall arrive later than in the interior. Inland climate may be either continental or semi-marine, depending on the direction of the wind.

Most Michigan soil is inherently acid and somewhat low in fertility. However, with the pH adjusted upwards and fertilizer added, it is quite productive.
**Lime** is not necessary unless a soil test indicates a pH of 5.7 or less. Most irrigation water used in Michigan contains enough lime to compensate for the naturally acid soil.

**Soil testing**
Crop and Soil Sciences Department
Michigan State University
East Lansing, Michigan 48824

**Recommended grasses.** According to lawn experts at Michigan State, mixtures of Kentucky bluegrass and fine fescues are the best for most parts of Michigan. Several varieties of Kentucky bluegrass have been tested under Michigan conditions and found to be quite good. They include: 'Baron,' 'Fylking,' 'Merion,' 'Nugget,' 'Adelphi,' and 'Bonnieblue.' If possible, a blend of three or more bluegrass varieties is preferable.

'Pennlawn,' 'Highlight,' 'Jamestown,' and 'Wintergreen' are among the varieties of fine fescue grown in Michigan.

The preferred time to seed is between August 15 and September 10 in southern Michigan, and between August 10 and September 1 in the northern part of the state.

**Publications office**
MSU Bulletin Office
P.O. Box 231
East Lansing, Michigan 48824
Out of state requests: Yes.

## WISCONSIN

**Soil and climate.** Wisconsin winters are cold and may reach—40°F. around Eau Claire and west-central parts of the state. Milwaukee winters are warmer and summers cooler due to the moderating influence of Lake Michigan. Summer thunderstorms are common. The wettest time of year is May to September.

Much of the soil in Wisconsin developed under an evergreen forest. Such soil is acid and generally low in nutrients. It must be adequately limed and fertilized for proper lawn growth.
**Lime** is often necessary.

**Soil testing**
Soil and Plant Analysis Laboratory
University of Wisconsin
806 S. Park Street
Madison, Wisconsin 53715, or,
State Soils Laboratory
Route 2
Marshfield, Wisconsin 54449

**Recommended grasses.** Blends of three or more Kentucky bluegrass varieties (see page 16) make a very handsome and hardy Wisconsin lawn. The fine fescues are used in sandy, dry soil or shady locations. Colonial bentgrass will sometimes make a good lawn (unmixed), especially along the lake shore.

**Publications office**
University of Wisconsin
Department of Agricultural Journalism
Agricultural Bulletin Building
1535 Observatory Drive
Madison, Wisconsin 53706
Out of state requests: Yes.

## MINNESOTA

**Soil and climate.** Minnesota's climate is continental. Temperatures can swing widely within a short time and summer rain is often abundant. In general, there is a tendency towards climatic extremes. Rainfall is generally more plentiful moving south and east.

Minnesota soil varies from sandy and sandy loam to heavy clay. Tests of lawn soil in the Twin Cities Area have shown that most are high in phosphorus.
**Lime** is usually applied every 6 to 10 years at rates of 50 to 150 pounds for every 1,000 square feet. The eastern half of the state commonly needs less liming. Make sure with a soil test.

**Soil testing**
Soil Testing Laboratory
University of Minnesota
St. Paul, Minnesota 55108

**Recommended grasses.** Most Minnesota lawns are either Kentucky bluegrass, red fescue, or a combination of the two. The more cold tolerant of the turf-type ryegrasses, such as 'NK-200,' are also used.

The bentgrasses are difficult to maintain. The coarse fescues make good lawns in transitional climates but lack tolerance to Minnesota's winters. Zoysiagrass is widely advertised but not adapted to Minnesota, since it requires a longer growing season.
**Publications office**
Bulletin Room
Coffey Hall
University of Minnesota
St. Paul, Minnesota 55108
Out of state requests: No.

## EAST CANADA

**Soil and climate.** This region includes the provinces of Manitoba, Nova Scotia, Ontario, and Quebec. For climate and soil specifics, read about the most northern states of the United States. Soil and climate will also be essentially the same.

**Lime.** Necessary in Nova Scotia and most of eastern Quebec, less so traveling westward. A soil test is the only way to know for sure.

**Soil testing**
Department of Soil Science
University of Manitoba

Winnipeg, Manitoba
R3T 2N2

Soils and Crops Branch
Nova Scotia Agricultural College
Truro, Nova Scotia
B2N 5E3

Department of Land Resource Science
Ontario Agricultural College
University of Guelph
Guelph, Ontario
N1G 2W1

Canadian Industries Limited
Soil Laboratory, Beloiel Works
McMasterville, Quebec

**Recommended grasses.** A good home lawn can be made throughout most of east Canada using a mixture of Kentucky bluegrass and creeping red fescue. Turf-type ryegrass may be included in such a mixture in order to speed establishment.

**Publications offices**
Contact the nearest Research Branch office of Agriculture Canada, a local provincial agricultural representative, or the Plant Science Department of a university for information about lawn growing in your area.

| | TOTAL INCHES RAIN | INCHES JULY/AUG. | JULY % SUNSHINE | DEC. % SUNSHINE | JULY DAYS ABOVE 90°F. | AVERAGE MAXIMUM/MINIMUM TEMPERATURES | | | | | | | | | | | |
|---|---|---|---|---|---|---|---|---|---|---|---|---|---|---|---|---|---|
| | | | | | | JAN. | FEB. | MARCH | APRIL | MAY | JUNE | JULY | AUG. | SEPT. | OCT. | NOV. | DEC. |

## MICHIGAN

| | | | | | | | | | | | | | | | | | |
|---|---|---|---|---|---|---|---|---|---|---|---|---|---|---|---|---|---|
| Alpena | 28 | 5.2 | 68 | 29 | 2 | 27/9 | 29/8 | 37/16 | 52/28 | 64/37 | 74/47 | 79/52 | 77/51 | 68/44 | 59/36 | 43/27 | 31/16 |
| Detroit | 31 | 6.0 | 70 | 32 | 6 | 32/19 | 34/20 | 43/28 | 58/39 | 68/48 | 79/59 | 83/63 | 82/62 | 74/55 | 63/45 | 48/34 | 35/24 |
| Flint | 30 | 6.2 | 70 | 32 | 2 | 30/15 | 32/15 | 41/24 | 56/35 | 67/44 | 77/55 | 81/58 | 80/57 | 72/50 | 62/40 | 46/31 | 34/20 |
| Grand Rapids | 32 | 5.6 | 66 | 24 | 5 | 30/16 | 33/16 | 42/24 | 57/36 | 69/45 | 79/56 | 83/60 | 82/58 | 74/51 | 63/41 | 46/31 | 34/21 |
| Lansing | 30 | 5.6 | 71 | 29 | 4 | 30/15 | 32/16 | 42/24 | 57/36 | 68/45 | 78/56 | 83/59 | 81/58 | 73/50 | 62/41 | 46/31 | 34/20 |
| Marquette | 31 | 6.1 | 67 | 28 | 2 | 25/12 | 26/13 | 34/20 | 48/32 | 59/41 | 70/50 | 75/57 | 74/57 | 65/49 | 56/41 | 40/29 | 29/18 |
| Muskegon | 32 | 5.1 | 68 | 30 | 1 | 30/18 | 31/18 | 40/25 | 55/36 | 66/45 | 76/55 | 80/60 | 79/59 | 71/52 | 61/42 | 46/33 | 34/23 |
| S. Ste. Marie | 32 | 5.7 | 63 | 28 | 1 | 22/6 | 24/7 | 32/15 | 47/29 | 59/38 | 70/47 | 75/52 | 73/53 | 64/46 | 55/38 | 39/26 | 27/13 |

## WISCONSIN

| | | | | | | | | | | | | | | | | | |
|---|---|---|---|---|---|---|---|---|---|---|---|---|---|---|---|---|---|
| Ashland | 30 | 8.3 | 64 | 41 | 3 | 13/-8 | 30/9 | 43/24 | 56/30 | 72/45 | 74/49 | 80/56 | 74/50 | 65/47 | 57/34 | 40/23 | 24/10 |
| Eau Claire | 29 | 7.5 | 68 | 44 | 4 | 9/-11 | 29/9 | 46/28 | 64/40 | 79/53 | 77/55 | 84/62 | 77/54 | 69/51 | 57/36 | 39/23 | 22/7 |
| Green Bay | 27 | 5.7 | 65 | 37 | 3 | 24/7 | 27/9 | 37/20 | 54/33 | 66/43 | 76/53 | 81/58 | 79/56 | 70/48 | 60/39 | 42/26 | 29/13 |
| Janesville | 32 | 7.3 | 69 | 40 | 14 | 16/-6 | 34/13 | 51/31 | 68/41 | 82/52 | 81/54 | 88/63 | 80/58 | 74/55 | 61/39 | 45/29 | 30/13 |
| La Crosse | 29 | 6.5 | 69 | 46 | 6 | 25/7 | 30/10 | 40/22 | 58/37 | 69/49 | 78/58 | 83/62 | 82/61 | 72/52 | 62/42 | 43/28 | 30/14 |
| Madison | 30 | 6.9 | 69 | 39 | 5 | 25/8 | 29/11 | 39/21 | 56/35 | 67/45 | 77/55 | 81/59 | 80/57 | 71/48 | 61/39 | 43/26 | 30/14 |
| Milwaukee | 29 | 6.1 | 71 | 38 | 4 | 27/11 | 30/15 | 39/23 | 55/35 | 65/43 | 75/54 | 80/59 | 80/59 | 71/51 | 61/41 | 44/28 | 31/17 |
| Wausau | 32 | 7.8 | 65 | 42 | 4 | 12/-8 | 29/9 | 44/27 | 61/37 | 78/52 | 74/52 | 82/61 | 75/54 | 66/51 | 57/37 | 39/25 | 24/9 |

## MINNESOTA

| | | | | | | | | | | | | | | | | | |
|---|---|---|---|---|---|---|---|---|---|---|---|---|---|---|---|---|---|
| Austin | 31 | 7.7 | 71 | 46 | 12 | 12/-10 | 25/5 | 49/32 | 67/43 | 80/56 | 82/56 | 87/63 | 78/55 | 74/50 | 59/36 | 42/24 | 23/10 |
| Duluth | 30 | 7.5 | 67 | 39 | 1 | 18/-1 | 22/2 | 33/14 | 48/29 | 60/39 | 70/48 | 76/55 | 74/54 | 64/45 | 54/36 | 35/21 | 22/6 |
| Fergus Falls | 25 | 6.4 | 72 | 49 | 4 | 4/-16 | 34/13 | 41/21 | 59/37 | 74/53 | 74/55 | 81/59 | 71/50 | 65/47 | 55/32 | 34/15 | 16/-3 |
| Inter. Falls | 26 | 7.3 | 46 | 33 | 2 | 13/-9 | 19/-5 | 32/9 | 49/27 | 62/38 | 72/48 | 78/53 | 75/51 | 64/42 | 54/33 | 32/17 | 18/-1 |
| Mpls/St. Paul | 26 | 6.7 | 71 | 40 | 7 | 21/3 | 26/7 | 37/20 | 55/35 | 68/46 | 77/57 | 82/61 | 81/60 | 71/49 | 61/39 | 41/24 | 27/11 |
| Rochester | 27 | 7.3 | 70 | 46 | 3 | 22/4 | 26/7 | 36/19 | 55/34 | 67/45 | 76/55 | 81/59 | 79/58 | 70/48 | 60/39 | 41/24 | 27/11 |
| St. Cloud | 27 | 7.1 | 72 | 48 | 4 | 19/-1 | 24/2 | 36/16 | 54/32 | 67/43 | 76/54 | 82/59 | 80/59 | 69/46 | 50/36 | 39/21 | 25/7 |

## EAST CANADA

AVERAGE DEGREES CELSIUS

| | | | | | | | | | | | | | | | | | |
|---|---|---|---|---|---|---|---|---|---|---|---|---|---|---|---|---|---|
| Frdrictn, N.B. | 43 | 6.9 | 234* | 91** | | -9.2 | -8.5 | -2.6 | 4.0 | 10.5 | 15.7 | 19.1 | 18.0 | 13.6 | 7.9 | 1.8 | -6.3 |
| Montrl, Que. | 39 | 7.3 | 264 | 77 | | -8.9 | -7.6 | -1.4 | 6.7 | 13.6 | 19.1 | 21.6 | 20.4 | 15.8 | 10.1 | 2.9 | -5.7 |
| No. Bay, Ont. | 38 | 7.4 | 267 | 70 | | -12.8 | -11.1 | -5.4 | 3.2 | 10.1 | 15.8 | 18.3 | 17.1 | 12.4 | 6.9 | -0.8 | -9.4 |
| Ottawa, Ont. | 33 | 6.4 | 277 | 78 | | -10.9 | -9.5 | -3.1 | 5.6 | 12.4 | 18.2 | 20.7 | 19.3 | 14.6 | 8.7 | 1.4 | -7.7 |
| Quebec, Que. | 43 | 8.3 | 233 | 65 | | -11.6 | -10.6 | -4.4 | 3.3 | 10.6 | 16.3 | 19.2 | 17.8 | 13.1 | 7.2 | 0.2 | -8.6 |
| St. Jhns, Nfld. | 59 | 7.7 | 213 | 52 | | -3.8 | -4.2 | -2.4 | 1.1 | 5.5 | 10.4 | 15.3 | 15.4 | 11.9 | 7.1 | 3.5 | -1.3 |
| Thndr By, Ont. | 29 | 6.3 | 302 | 92 | | -14.8 | -13.0 | -6.2 | 2.4 | 8.3 | 13.8 | 17.5 | 16.5 | 11.3 | 6.1 | -2.5 | -10.8 |
| Toronto, Ont. | 31 | 5.8 | 281 | 77 | | -4.4 | -3.8 | 0.6 | 7.6 | 13.2 | 19.2 | 21.8 | 21.1 | 17.0 | 11.2 | 4.8 | -1.8 |

*Total hours bright sun, July    **Total hours bright sun, December.

# Lawn calendar

Temperatures control the timetable but not the calendar. However, we must use the calendar to express time. The North is a large and diverse area. For example, temperatures in the Midwest and North for the month of March range from 31° in Duluth, Minnesota, to 56° in Louisville, Kentucky.

## Climate comparisons of 18 cities:

| cities | number of days growing season | average last frost | average first frost |
|---|---|---|---|
| Duluth, MN | 125 | 5/22 | 9/24 |
| Bismark, ND | 136 | 5/11 | 9/24 |
| Marquette, ME | 159 | 5/13 | 10/19 |
| North Platte, NE | 160 | 4/30 | 10/7 |
| Green Bay, WI | 161 | 5/6 | 10/13 |
| Minneapolis/ St. Paul, MN | 166 | 4/30 | 10/13 |
| Sioux City, IA | 169 | 4/27 | 10/13 |
| Peoria, IL | 181 | 4/22 | 10/20 |
| Detroit, MI | 182 | 4/21 | 10/20 |
| Springfield, IL | 186 | 4/20 | 10/23 |
| Pittsburgh, PA | 187 | 4/20 | 10/23 |
| Grand Rapids, MI | 190 | 4/23 | 10/30 |
| Cincinnati, OH | 192 | 4/15 | 10/25 |
| Charleston, WV | 193 | 4/18 | 10/28 |
| Springfield, MO | 201 | 4/12 | 10/30 |
| Evansville, IN | 216 | 4/2 | 11/4 |
| Louisville, KY | 220 | 4/1 | 11/7 |

The high and low temperatures for each month, total inches rainfall, July-August rainfall, percent of July and December sunshine, and days in July are listed for 158 towns beginning on page 80. Let them be your timetable guide.

## January-February

**Snowmold:** Take advantage of a mid-winter thaw to treat a lawn that showed damage from this disease last spring.

## March-April

Where temperatures are favorable for lawn growth, such as in Kentucky, West Virginia, and Maryland, begin planting and fertilizing.

**Spring patching & rolling:** If you live in an area where the ground is still frozen or covered with light snow, seeds already planted won't sprout, but will as soon as temperatures rise. In established lawns after the spring thaw, roll fall-seeded lawns and areas raised by frost with a half-filled roller.

**New lawns:** Fall and spring are good times to start a lawn. The cool-season grasses, Kentucky bluegrass, fescue, bentgrass and ryegrass, find temperatures of 70° to 75°F. ideal for growth. If seeding is done when the temperatures are favorable, lawns will become established quickly, overcoming much of the competition from weeds and avoiding erosion from heavy spring rains.

**Sodding:** This can be done any time during the growing season, though spring and fall are ideal for quick establishment.

**Fertilizing:** If you missed fertilizing your lawn last fall, do it this spring as soon as temperatures reach about 60°F.

**Dethatching:** Thatch slows air and water penetration, harbors pests and diseases, and slows growth by insulating roots and crowns against warming spring temperatures. Your lawn will recover in the shortest time from dethatching when temperatures are above 70°F. and the grass is growing vigorously.

*Dethatching rake: Good for small lawns.*

**Aerification:** Early spring is a fine time to perform this chore. It opens up the soil, providing roots with more water and air. If done prior to fertilizing, nutrients will reach the root zone quickly for spring green-up.

**Crabgrass:** You can do your lawn a big favor if it was bothered by crabgrass last summer. Crabgrass seeds left over from last year will start to sprout when temperatures reach 65° to 70°F. for four to five consecutive days. You can stop these seeds from coming up by applying a pre-emergent barrier *before* seeds germinate. Timing is important. If you plan to do any spring seeding, look for the word Tupersan (sideron) on the label. This product will not harm germinating grass seed.

**Broadleaf weeds:** Blooming dandelions are a sure sign of weeds, but other broadleaf weeds that aren't as obvious can be just as troublesome; plantain and knotweed among others. There are two good reasons to control them now. First, they are most susceptible to herbicides when young and actively growing. And second, weed killers developed for their control, work efficiently in warm weather.

**Grubs:** As the soil warms up, grubs move up to the root zone from deep winter burrows. Treat them with an insecticide such as diazinon. Be patient, insecticides move slowly through root zone. Follow label directions carefully.

**Disease:** The cool, moist weather of spring favors development of several diseases. Leaf spot is a problem with bluegrass. Look for it in fall as well as spring. A healthy lawn will usually make a strong comeback as weather warms.

Stripe-smut symptoms are most pronounced during early to late spring, and again during similar periods of fall. Symptoms are almost non-existent during mid-summer. Dollar spot can occur anytime from now until late summer, especially when temperatures are up into the 80's and humidity is high.

## May

**Feeding:** If you think heavy rains have washed out nutrients, now is the time for a second application of fertilizer. May can be the first month for feeding if a heavy application of fertilizer was applied in the fall. Fertilize zoysia and bermudagrass as they begin to green. Their best growing period is just ahead and early feeding speeds recovery from winter dormancy. It also gives you a head start on weeds preventing their growth. If you overseeded the lawn last winter, don't add fertilizer for awhile. Feeding now would only prolong the life of the overseeded winter grass.

**Planting:** When temperatures reach the mid-70's, sprigging and plugging weather has arrived in areas where bermuda and zoysiagrass are adapted. The hot weather ahead makes this the best time of year to plant these grasses.

**Overseeding bermudagrass:** If you've overseeded your bermuda-grass lawn (zoysiagrass doesn't lend

*Spring mowing for cool-season grasses.*

itself well to this practice) now is the time to discourage the winter grass. Start mowing lower, less than 1 inch, to allow warmth and light to reach the bermudagrass.

## June

**Feeding:** Any feeding should be done early in the month, before your cool-season grass begins to go dormant. During dormancy, grasses live off stored nutrients, while actually manufacturing very little. Continue feeding bermuda and zoysiagrass through the growing season until temperatures fall below 70°F. and your lawn begins to grow very slowly.

**Crabgrass:** If you didn't treat your lawn with a pre-emergent weed killer in the spring, crabgrass should make itself evident by now. Various sprays are available for selective control of crabgrass. Apply them as soon as crabgrass is noticed and keep the soil moist.

**Insects:** This month sod webworms may begin to cause irregular brown patches in the lawn. You'll probably see the adult moths fluttering around close to the lawn at dusk. Actually, the night-feeding larvae do the damage. Armyworms also show up in summer. They're about twice as large as webworms and feed on the grass in broad daylight.

Chinch bugs are especially bad in warm dry weather in the Northeast. Discovering them is the first step towards control (See page 69.) Hunt near the damaged area. Normal hatching times are often the first week in June and August.

**Disease:** Leaf spot disease continues to be a problem in southern areas. Brown patch is severe in hot weather. High humidity and temperatures of 60° to 80°F. are favorable for its development.

## July-August

**Watering:** It is the nature of cool-season grasses to go dormant in summer. Some people like it that way, but if you want to keep your lawn green, see pages 34 to 39 for instructions.

**Fertilizing:** July and August is not the best time to fertilize cool-season grasses. Warm-season bermuda and zoysiagrass, however, are growing most vigorously and may require additional nutrients.

**Planting:** The middle of August to the middle of September is one of the best times to reseed an old lawn, or plant a new one. Summer's heat will bring the seed quickly and the cooler weather that is soon to follow will relieve you of frequent watering.

**Pests and diseases:** A light case of brown patch can injure top growth, but the lawn should make a quick recovery in a few weeks if temperatures drop. If disease-favoring weather continues, so will brown patch. Chemical control may be necessary. In the Northeast, the small black and red chinch bug may have hatched a second generation, so be on the lookout. Continue to spot-treat crabgrass as it appears.

**Grubs:** In mid-summer, adult beetles lay their eggs in the lawn. The tiny, white grubs that hatch from these eggs feed near the surface until the first cold spell. Then they burrow into the surface more than a foot deep for overwintering. Control is most effective on surface-feeding young grubs.

## September

Cooler nights bring greater pleasure and fewer problems with lawn care. Grasses take on new life after the hard times of summer.

**Broadleafs:** Now is a good time to begin controlling vigorously growing weeds. Young weeds are more susceptible to chemical control. Remember too, that chemicals designed for their control work best in warm but not hot weather.

**Planting and dethatching:** Planting weather, the year's best, continues into this month. And as grasses perk up, the chore of thatch removal should be considered while favorable weather ensures quick recovery.

**Overseeding bermudagrass:** Overseed bermudagrass this month, as cooling weather favors germination and development of your winter grass and discourages further growth of the bermudagrass. Mow first, then

rake and mow again, removing the clippings. Rake seeds into the lawn and keep moist until they come up.

**Fertilizer and lime:** Discover the great response you get from a fall application of fertilizer. A lawn fed now spends less effort on top growth, more on root build-up. The result is a sturdier lawn going into winter and a stronger start next spring.

A fall application of lime is washed by rains down into the soil, where it is needed. Winter freezing and thawing further help the process.

**Disease and weeds:** Cool moist weather can bring problems, especially for Kentucky bluegrass, in the form of leaf spot disease. As in spring, it is the cool, moist weather that favors development.

*Fall: Time to fertilize cool-season lawns.*

## October-November

Where weather permits, the great opportunities of last month — planting, feeding, and weed killing — carry over for at least the first half of October.

If snowmold gave you trouble last spring, take precautions in November so it won't return. The disease organisms are still present; snow supplies the moisture to activate them. Infected grass develops patches several inches to several feet wide. Grass blades tend to form a mat or crust, and may show white to pink, or grey to black mold. Control once after first frost (sometime in mid-winter) when there is no snow on the ground, and again after snow melts next spring.

## Summary

Only through experience can you get a perfect timetable. However, each chore has a best time — "the time that is most effective." Taking another look at our timetable, we see that it's spring-summer-fall, though it's "your date" in spring, "your date" in summer, and "your date" in fall.

# Lawn tips

A book about lawns is never complete. Here are some miscellaneous tips, some from previous chapters, designed to serve as handy information in a concentrated form.

## Trees in the lawn

Grade changes can kill many trees. Piling soil around the trunk can suffocate surface roots. Removing soil either damages roots or exposes them to drying. During the establishment of a lawn, any grade changes around trees should be gradual. Changes of more than a couple of inches require the use of retaining walls or dry walls, which are best extended to the dripline of the tree.

Some trees especially adapted to growing in northern lawns include:

| | |
|---|---|
| *Acer* spp. | Maple |
| *Betula* spp. | Birch |
| *Cercis canadensis* | Redbud |
| *Chioanthus* spp. | Fringe tree |
| *Cornus* spp. | Dogwood |
| *Crataegus* spp. | Hawthorne |
| *Koelreuteria* spp. | Golden-rain tree |
| *Magnolia* spp. | Magnolia |
| *Pyrus* spp. | Pear |

Instead of a lawn, ground covers can be grown under trees. If the shade is more than 50 percent, ground covers are a better solution than turf.

## Treat the cause, not the symptom

If a trouble spot develops, search, then treat the cause, not the symptom. Here are some examples:

A dry spot that appears repeatedly in the lawn may result from a lack of organic matter, or improper grading. Not enough depth to the soil above bedrock, or buried concrete or debris will also cause drying.

**Moss:** If you have a problem with moss, there are temporary cures, but for a permanent solution, look for the cause. Moss is usually the result of improper drainage and shade, not soil acidity. Other factors contributing to moss are poor air circulation and insufficient light, which slow the evaporation of water from the soil.

Copper sulfate at three tablespoons per 1,000 square feet or ammonium sulfate at 10 pounds per 1,000 square feet are controls which may be used. Be aware, however, this amount of ammonia sulfate may furnish too much nitrogen for cool-season grasses if applied in late spring. (Also, specialty fertilizers containing ferrous and ferric ammonium sulfate will control moss.)

**Mushrooms:** After prolonged periods of wet weather, you may notice mushrooms coming up in the lawn. This often indicates the presence of construction debris or old tree roots and stumps that are decaying below the surface. It may be years after construction before the mushrooms appear. There is no effective chemical control for these fungi and they cause no damage to the turf. However, if you feel they are unsightly and poisonous, remove them with the lawn mower or a bamboo rake.

**Moles:** A single mole can range over several acres, digging several thousand feet of tunnels. The structure of the surface tunnels and the temporary way in which they are used makes mole control difficult. Gases introduced into these tunnels are ineffective because they will quickly diffuse through the thin overhead sod covering. Since moles are primarily carnivorous, it is difficult to poison them. The most practical control is to trap the animal, which can be very time consuming, or to remove their food supply so that they migrate elsewhere. Until their primary food source, grubs and earthworms, is eliminated, moles will continue to move in to feed. If you have moles, the best solution is to treat for grubs.

## Grooming

Edging with a border of wood, stone or concrete, makes maintenance less of a chore. A mower is then able to ride over the edging, which reduces hand trimming. A lawn will always look its best and those troublesome creeping grasses can be kept from climbing into flower borders. The use of wood can be as simple as laying a 1x4 or 2x4 on edge. Bricks in a row or a band of concrete four to five inches wide are other solutions.

## Leaves on the lawn

There are leaves that easily blow away and there are leaves that are big and determined to stay on your lawn. Some trees drop their leaves in a short time while others seem to drop forever. Regardless of when and how they fall, rake them up and add them to the compost pile. They will decay faster if they're shredded. Leaves do not act like a blanket to keep the grass warm. They actually smother the lawn, especially when it's wet, thus depriving the grass of light.

## Lawn clippings as a mulch

If you use lawn clippings as a compost or mulch in the vegetable garden, take care that the lawn clippings are free of 2,4-D, and other broadleaf weed killers. 2,4-D effects plants in various ways. Continuous mulching of tomatoes with treated clippings has resulted in distorted plants. Let clippings treated with 2,4-D settle into the lawn, or discard.

## Spring cleanup

These are the steps for a spring clean-up and quick green-up of cool-season grasses.

**1.** Break up an ice covering that may have been coating the lawn for a long time. Do not walk on frosted turf.

**2.** The lawn should be cleaned of winter debris. Use a rake for clean-up.

*When you see mushrooms in the lawn, it usually means there is decaying debris below the soil surface. See above for treatment.*

**3.** Spread seed at a rate of 3 pounds per 1,000 square feet for bare spots, a quarter of that for thin areas.

**4.** Follow the seeding with an application of Tupersan for crabgrass control. Read the label. This application will not injure the seed you have just planted. Other crabgrass controls prevent germination of all grass seeds.

## Mow less often

Recently tested growth regulators have displayed the ability to slow lawngrass growth for 5 to 8 weeks. Lawns are mowed only half as often when the chemicals are used.

Several difficulties prevent marketing for home use at this time: 1. The regulators work best only on single-grass lawns. 2. Slowed growth may favor weeds and disease. 3. Weather, stage of growth, fertility status, and time of application all effect results. 4. Improper application can cause damage to the lawn. Presently available growth regulators are best adapted for difficult or impossible mowing situations; along fences, walls, or on steep, unmowable slopes, for example.

## Lawn colorants

Warm-season lawns, browned by winter dormancy, can be successfully colored with green dyes or latex paints. This is an alternative to overseeding with a cool-season grass.

We quote the Cooperative Extension Association of Nassau County in New York.

"Several experiment stations have been trying out various paints and dyes on brown grass with many results. Many of these dyes are now on the market. Dyes can be used on summer lawns, browned from summer heat or lack of water, or in winter on browned zoysia or bermudagrass. Most dyes that have been tested are non-toxic to animals and plants. No harmful soil residuals have been found to date. Variations have been found in lasting ability and color. For best results:

**1.** Apply a fine mist with pressure sprayers, not hose types.

**2.** Apply to brown dormant grass, not growing grass.

**3.** Allow dyes to dry for several hours before rain or watering grass.

**4.** Apply to neatly trimmed lawns — not unmowed areas."

## Paving block lawns

Concrete paving blocks combined with turfgrass will produce a new kind of multi-use lawn area. Paving blocks, available from many manufacturers, can be used in driveways, parking areas, or pathways. They are similar in appearance to oversized checkerboards, with alternating squares of supportive blocks and planting holes. An average block covers about three square feet. Standard concrete building blocks can also be used.

Planting a lawn with paving blocks is a simple operation. If the proposed area will be required to support heavy weight, such as a driveway, a solid base for the blocks should be prepared. The paving blocks are placed in position side by side, and the holes filled with a quality soil. Seed or sod plugs can then be planted, the same as for any new lawn.

There are many advantages to this type of lawn. They are naturally more attractive than bare soil or artificial surface, and are cooler and produce less glare. During the rainy season water runoff is less due to the lawn's greater absorption qualities. Different grass types produce different effects. A vertically growing grass such as tall fescue will obscure the blocks completely. A horizontal grass such as bermuda will stay low, allowing some of the paving block to remain exposed, providing a textured pattern.

The cost of a paving block lawn will of course vary with the situation. As a general rule, however, it should be the same or even less than poured concrete.

## Changing grade

Even after a lawn is established, you may want to change the grade to correct water run-off or level high and low areas. Grass will grow with the addition of small amounts of sand, organic matter, and top soil. You will find change of grade is simpler if you go at it gradually, adding or subtracting a little fill at a time.

## Washboard effect

Turfgrass areas regularly cut with a power mower may develop wave-like ridges running at right angles to the direction of mowing. Alternating directions of cut will help correct these ridges.

## Cautions

Read the label every time you spray or dust and pay attention to cautions and warnings. Mix sprays on a solid level surface to lessen spillage. Avoid spilling pesticides on the skin or clothing and wash exposed areas thoroughly with soap and water. Do not eat or smoke while spraying. Keep all chemicals out of reach of children. Store them in a locked cabinet or high on a shelf. Set aside a special set of mixing tools, measuring spoons, and graduated measuring cups. Use them for measuring and mixing sprays only. Be sure to keep all chemicals in their original, labeled containers. Store lawn fertilizers combined with weed killers, separately from garden fertilizers to prevent accidental misuse.

*Turf block lawns provide a cool, attractive alternative to concrete or asphalt driveways. The weight of the car is supported by the blocks, and not the sod.*

# Index

# Tables and conversions

The lawn keeper is asked to be a measurer in almost every operation — "Apply 2# of nitrogen per 1000 square feet," "Mix two tablespoons per gallon," "Spread two or three inches of organic matter over the soil." "Determine the area of your lawn," "Add lime if soil tests show the need." In these directions we find the elements "How much," "How wide," "How long."

**So you are about to measure the area of your lawn.** Once the area is measured write it down for future reference.

## Charts and tables index

There are many charts and tables distributed throughout this book. All have been designed to simplify and categorize the sometimes technical information that is needed to understand lawn growth and lawn care.

## How many square feet?

**Irregular shapes**
(within 5% accuracy)
Measure a long (L) axis of the area. At every 10 feet on the length line measure the width at right angles to the length line. Total all widths and multiply by 10.

**Area = (A₁ A₂ + B₁ B₂ + C₁ C₂ etc.) x 10**

$$A = (40' + 60' + 32') \times 10$$
$$A = 132' \times 10'$$
$$A = 1,320 \text{ square feet}$$

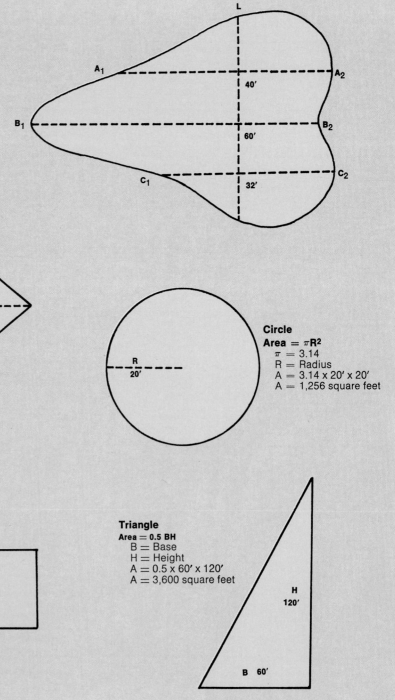

**Unusual shapes**
Calculations can be made by sections and totaled.

In this case calculate and add together:

　　Area of triangle
　　Area of rectangle
　　One-half area of circle

TOTAL = square feet in area

**Circle**
**Area = πR²**
　π = 3.14
　R = Radius
　A = 3.14 x 20' x 20'
　A = 1,256 square feet

**Triangle**
Area = 0.5 BH
　B = Base
　H = Height
　A = 0.5 x 60' x 120'
　A = 3,600 square feet

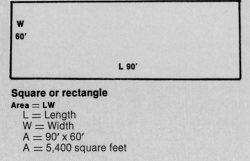

**Square or rectangle**
Area = LW
　L = Length
　W = Width
　A = 90' x 60'
　A = 5,400 square feet